Andrew Carnegie

MR. CARNEGIE IN' HIS LIBRARY,
DICTATING TO HIS SECRETARY

Andrew Carnegie

Reedited, and republished by Ultimate Brainstorming.

www.UltimateBrainstorming.com

ISBN-13:
978-1522995500

ISBN-10:
1522995501

Andrew Carnegie

The Man and His Work

By

Bernard Alderson

Andrew Carnegie

PREFACE

A KEYNOTE to the true description of a rich man who does good with his money is struck by Ruskin when he defines wealth to be "the possession of the valuable by the valiant"; for, as he goes on to say, "that man is the richest who, having perfected the function of his own life, has also the widest helpful interest."

These words apply with singular fitness to Andrew Carnegie. The story of his life is a record of high aims and strenuous endeavor, disclosing constant indications of a master mind; so that the rising generation, as they follow the gradual growth of his fortunes, and the development of his character, may gather from an account of the winning of his wealth a strong incentive to courageous enterprise, and also appreciate the intention of his pithy paradox, "A man who dies rich dies disgraced?"

Who can fail to admire that firm purpose to complete his duties as he interprets them, which has reached a noble climax in the fixed determination to put his millions to the most beneficial use? He is anxious above all things to prevent this mint of money from doing harm, by disbursing it worthily during his lifetime, and although he must accept the penalties with the pleasures of his prominent position, he can well afford to disregard petty criticism.

"Wealth," said Gladstone, "is the business of the world"; and when he added, "the enormous power which it possesses has been used on the whole well," we cannot doubt that he had in his mind this great millionaire for whom he frequently expressed a warm regard, and whose "Gospel of Wealth" he reviewed in the glowing terms which are quoted in these pages.

Mr. Carnegie, himself a thorough and thoughtful student of men and manners, is heartily at one with an old writer who has quaintly asserted that "to amass money and to make no use of it is as senseless as to hunt game and not roast it," and therefore it is one of the main purposes of this volume to prove that he - " the self-made Steel King - stands head and shoulders above most of his fellow-millionaires, in that he has undertaken to distribute with his own hands, and at his own discretion after most careful thought, the gigantic funds which he has accumulated by such alert and unflinching industry; holding himself to be no more than a trustee, responsible for their application through such channels, and to such ends, as may be expected to enrich the minds and moral welfare of those whom he thus makes his heirs.

CONTENTS

LIST OF ILLUSTRATIONS

Chapter I

Birthplace and Boyhood

ANDREW CARNEGIE was born in Dunfermline on November 25, 1837, the year in which Queen Victoria ascended the throne. Dunfermline is one of Scotland's oldest cities, and has been the scene of many famous episodes in Scottish history. It formerly contained one of the richest abbeys in the land, but to-day only the nave of the church remains among the ruins. In this abbey the renowned Malcolm and his consort and seven other Scottish kings and five queens are buried. Adjacent to its ruins are those of the ancient royal palace in which the hapless Charles I. was born. What, however, endears Dunfermline above everything else to Andrew Carnegie is not the fact that it was the burial-place or the residence of Scottish royalty, but that Robert Bruce was here laid to rest in his "winding-sheet of cloth of gold."

Young Carnegie early began to study the history of his native land, and it was not long before he became a hero-worshiper of the most pronounced type. Bruce, Wallace and Bums were exalted by his youthful patriotism to lofty thrones of veneration; the stricken fields of Bannockbum and Stirling became to him a glorious heritage. These democratic feelings of national enthusiasm were intensified by the circumstances of the period. For many years Scotland had suffered under a tyrannical system of government, which had created a feeling of bitter hatred against the landed aristocracy. Kings and nobles were looked upon as mere puppets, and held in common detestation by the rank and file. A succession of weak sovereigns had occupied the English throne, and by their unwise actions had alienated the loyalty of the Scottish people.

These facts were early impressed on young Andrew's mind by his uncle, who took care that the boy should have a proper conception of Scottish history. Andrew attended the local school, but the chief part of his education was given him by his uncle, a man of some ability, who held extreme democratic republican views, which he expressed with unrestrained vigor.

Mr. Carnegie says that his political instincts were first aroused by listening to the speeches of his uncle and father, who addressed in the evenings large assemblies of the people. They were the leaders of an agitation for reform, and in the course of their speeches they fearlessly denounced the oppression of the English Government. These sentiments found fertile soil in young Andrew's mind. Many years afterward he said:-

"What we learn at seven sticks! When I was at that age, I awoke one night to hear my uncle had been put into jail. I knew there was hidden in the attic a rebellious republican flag, for all our family were Chartists, and to this day when I speak of a king or hereditary privilege my blood tingles and mounts to my face. Sometimes - and not so many years ago - I have felt for a passing moment that to shoot all hereditary kings, one after the other, would not be uncongenial work, for I hate hereditary privileges with a hate nothing else inspires, because I got it at seven, and it requires an effort to keep it within bounds."

One of the proudest boasts he makes to-day is that his uncle was imprisoned for upholding the rights of the people, and vindicating the liberty of free speech.

For eleven years, during the most impressionable period of his life, Andrew Carnegie breathed this atmosphere so strongly charged with republican sentiment. The lessons of that early training were firmly ingrained upon his mind, and forty years afterward we find the natural result in his book, "Triumphant Democracy." The seeds sown in his boyhood were destined to produce enduring fruit. His antipathy to royalty and the aristocracy has been to him a consuming passion. The environment of his youth, and his residence in the United States, have been chiefly responsible for this uncompromising attitude.

But the condition and general welfare of the masses, when Andrew Carnegie was a boy, were vastly different from what they are to-day. He has learned much since his youth, and now regards Great Britain as a republic, like the United States, with this distinction, that the one is crowned, the other uncrowned. It is only after years of wise monarchical government that the Scottish people have become animated with that loyal devotion to the throne which is now one of their distinguishing characteristics.

Andrew Carnegie's political convictions were thus formed by his uncle, but his character and habits were most happily moulded by his mother. She was a typical specimen of the strong-minded, warm-hearted, frugal Scottish housewife. Until Andrew was eight years old she attended to his education and taught him the rudiments. He was then handed over to the care of the local schoolmaster. Here is an amusing incident of his school life, which throws some light on the way in which he was brought up.

Every morning the lessons were preceded by some religious exercises, and upon one occasion each member of the class had to repeat a proverb from the Bible. When it came to Andrew's turn he stood up and boldly proclaimed, "Take care of your pence, the pounds will take care of themselves." This was not quite orthodox, but it illustrated how the famous maxim had been drilled into the lad's mind by his mother.

Andrew Carnegie must be included in the long list of illustrious men whose success in life has been largely due to the greatest of all blessings a youth can have - a wise and good mother. His devotion to her was exceedingly strong. She was the guardian angel of his life-his "saint," as he always called her. In every trouble and sorrow she was his helper and comforter, and in every difficulty and perplexity his guide and counselor. Her strong loving influence supported him through all the severe strain of his strenuous druggie for success. It was her practical sympathy and cheerful encouragement which sustained his youthful strength and ambition during the darkest days. Never for one moment has he forgotten what she did for him. He has often said he can never adequately estimate all that he owes to her strong will, her far-seeing judgment, and her loving, motherly sympathy.

When he became possessed of great wealth she still remained his constant companion, and accompanied him on all his holidays, both at borne and abroad.

While she lived he remained single, choosing to lavish upon her all the love and reverence of his nature. Now that she has passed away, he is never tired of singing her praises and of recalling her goodness. This deep attachment and unbroken fidelity to his mother is one of the strongest features of Andrew Carnegie's character, and herein he has set a worthy example to every youth who desires to become a true man.

His mother, he once remarked, was the mainspring of all his hopes. For her he worked, for her sake alone he sought to acquire wealth, so that her old age might be spent in comfort and in peace. To his great joy she lived to the ripe old age of eighty. The little homestead at Dunfermline derived its livelihood from the staple industry of the town. Andrew's father was a master weaver, and as the owner of four damask looms and an employer of apprentices he was looked upon as a prosperous business man. Those were the days of the hand looms, when the trade in cloth was done through merchants, who issued their orders to master weavers and supplied them with the raw material.

The introduction of the steam loom effected a complete change in these conditions. The old methods could not successfully compete with the new steam loom and the factory system of labor. This trade revolution cast a shadow over Mr. Carnegie's home and future prospects. His business rapidly dwindled, and eventually became unprofitable. For a time he struggled manfully against these adverse forces, but he had at last to give way.

One day he returned from delivering some goods to say that he could get no further orders, and tuning to his children he said, "Andy, I have no more work." It is in the irony of things that the youngster should have felt in his boyhood the cruel effect of those forces of competition and enterprise of which, in later years, he was to be the stanchest champion, and which were destined to bring him such enormous wealth.

"No more work!" The keen-witted boy knew what that meant, and the news, with all its significance and unspeakable misery, sank deep into his childish heart. He there and then resolved that he would strive with all his strength to drive the wolf of poverty from his home. It was but the impetuous resolution of a boy of ten, yet it was the spark of a strong determination which had suddenly been kindled in his nature, and which never ceased to exert its influence, urging him on through many youthful trials to ultimate success.

Andrew's father was placed in a difficult position. It was useless to move to another town, for the same conditions prevailed everywhere. A family council was held, and it was decided, after some hesitation, to follow the example of some relatives, who, a few years before, had emigrated to Pittsburgh, America, where they had met with encouraging success.

The parents, no doubt, could have managed very well in the old country, but for the sake of their two boys they decided to take all the risks and endure all the hardships of emigration. The crossing of the Atlantic in the sailing vessels of those days was a rough experience, and the discomforts of a journey from New York to Pittsburgh were by no means insignificant. Such considerations, however, did not weigh much with these hardy Scotch folk.

The hand looms and the business were sold and preparations made for the long voyage. The wrench from their native town, and the breaking up of their home and friendly associations, proved very hard and trying; and in after years Andrew Carnegie gave proof of his attachment to his birthplace when he said: "What Benares is to the Hindoo, Mecca to the Mohammedan, Jerusalem to the Christian, all that and more Dunfermline is to me."

In 1848, the year of the overthrow of kingship in France, this young king-hater and his family set sail for the republic across the Atlantic. The little party - father, mother, Andrew, and his younger brother Tom - embarked at Broomielaw, Glasgow, on the 800-ton sailing vessel Wiscassett, and thus entered upon their seven weeks' voyage to the land of promise - poor emigrants, in quest of fortune. Little did they think as they saw the shores of bonnie Scotland receding in the distance that some day one of their number would return from the quest and "bring his sheaves with him."

Young Andy had plenty of time to find his sea legs, and he thoroughly enjoyed the voyage, and the liking for the sea then awakened has always remained one of his greatest delights. He was only eleven years old at the time, but he has distinct recollections of that parting from the old country and the launch out into a new life in the Western world.

The family reached Pittsburgh safely, and immediately settled down. Mr. Carnegie obtained work at a cotton factory in the town, and when twelve years old Andrew began his business career as a bobbin boy at a dollar and twenty cents a week. The fact that he could now contribute toward the family expenses filled him with intense satisfaction.

"I was no longer," he writes, "dependent upon my parents, but at last admitted to the family partnership as a contributing member, and able to help them. I think this makes a man out of a boy sooner than anything else - and a real man, too, if there be any germ of true manliness in him. It is everything to feel that you are useful. I have had to deal with great sums, many millions of dollars have since passed through my hands, but putting all these together, and considering money-making as a means of pleasure-giving, or of that other feeling much deeper than pleasure- of genuine satisfaction, I tell you that one dollar and twenty cents outweighs all. It was the direct reward of honest manual labor; it represented a week of very hard work - so hard that, but for the aim and end which sanctified it, slavery might not be too strong a term to describe it."

His hours for one so young were exceedingly long, and it is no wonder he has retained such a vivid recollection of the hardships of child labor. Prom early mom till dewy eve-from dark to dark-with but an interval of forty minutes for his dinner, he slaved away at his uncongenial task. His next situation proved even more laborious and responsible, and nothing but strong determination and persistent ambition could have stood the test. His work was to fire the boiler and run the steam-engine which drove the machinery of a small factory. For a boy of thirteen this was, indeed, an onerous position, and the heavy strain of the work soon began to affect his health and to tell upon his nerves. Even in his sleep he was haunted by the dread possibility of calamity, and during the night would vaguely reach forth his hand to test the water-gauge. One false move he knew might cause the whole place to be blown to atoms.

Those were dark days for the young aspirant, but he had not a thought of burdening his home with his troubles. Cheerfulness almost amounted to a religion V in that little household, and each member strove to put aside all disturbing thoughts. He was blessed with a spirit of keen, dogged determination. The flame of his ambition - most precious of gifts - burned brightly within him, and although his surroundings must have filled him with despair, he never showed the white flag, but always had confidence in his future. "I was young and had my dreams; and something within me always told me that this would not last, and that I should soon get into a better position." With *Nil desperandum* for his motto, he became a confirmed and plucky little optimist.

The other members of his family, including his mother, were toiling hard, but when they gathered together in the evenings all showed their brightest spirits, and kept their personal worries and sorrows to themselves. His home was a very happy one, full of sweetness and love, and to this day he cherishes its memories.

"I always pity the sons and daughters of rich men," he said many years afterward, "who are attended by servants, and have governesses at a later age, but they do not know what they have missed. They have fathers and mothers - and very kind fathers and mothers too - and they think that they enjoy the sweetness of these blessings to the full, but this they cannot do; for the poor boy who has in his father his constant companion, tutor and model, and in his mother -holy name- his nurse, teacher, guardian angel, saint, all in one, has a richer, more precious fortune in life than any rich man's son can possibly know, and compared with which all other fortunes count for little. It is because I know how sweet and happy and pure the home of honest poverty is, how free from care, from quarrels, how loving and united its members, that I sympathize with the rich man's boy and congratulate the poor man's boy; and it is for these reasons that from the ranks of the poor the great and good have always sprung, and always must spring. It seems nowadays a matter of universal desire that poverty should be abolished. We should be quite willing to abolish luxury, but to abolish poverty would be to destroy the only soil upon which mankind can depend to produce those virtues which can alone enable our race to reach a still higher civilization than it now possesses."

Andrew Carnegie

CHAPTER II

STEPPING-STONES

ANDREW CARNEGIE is not an example to quote in illustration of the proverb, " A rolling stone gathers no moss." He has referred with scorn to the precept, "Stick to your last," which he seems to think equivalent to "Stick in the mud," and therefore not the motto he would recommend to a youth who desires to make progress.

At fourteen he made his third change, and forsook the dismal task of stoking for the healthier and brighter work of a telegraph boy. This was his first step forward, which he was able to take through the kindness of Mr. J. Douglas Reed, a Dunfermline gentleman who had gone out to the States early in life and made a name for himself in the telegraph service. When he heard that Mr. Carnegie's family had also come from far-off Dunfermline, he promised the father that he would give "Andy" a berth, and during the whole time he was in the telegraph service he did all he could to help him forward.

The changed conditions and healthy environment of his new work filled "Andy" with the greatest happiness. He was like a caged bird set free. Penned up as he had been in the reeking atmosphere of an engine room, a life in the open air seemed an ideal existence. It was, he said, "a transference from the darkness to light, from the desert to paradise."

When he found himself amidst books and newspapers, and was privileged to use pen and ink in the course of his daily round, the common task immediately began to glow with promise, and he considered himself in his new sphere the happiest boy alive. This youthful joy was the first evidence of the strong attachment Mr. Carnegie has always shown for figures and writing. A telegraph office is not the place where one would expect to find the germs of literary inspiration, but it was while carrying out the duties of telegraph messenger that young Carnegie first entertained the hope of someday writing articles and books himself.

Having secured this congenial position, with a salary of three dollars a week, he was greatly troubled lest he should lose it. He entered upon his new work with two drawbacks: his health had been impaired by the strain of his former occupation, and he was unacquainted with the commercial quarters of the city - a defect which he feared would hinder him in making his deliveries. So he set himself to remedy it without delay, and eventually overcame the difficulty by calling into use his excellent memory. With characteristic determination he resolved to learn by heart the names of all the business houses in the principal streets. Soon he was able to shut his eyes and repeat in correct order the names of the firms on one side of the street and of those on the other. "Then," he says, "I felt safe."

When he had successfully overcome this difficulty another presented itself. One of the duties of a telegraph boy in those primitive days was to climb the poles whenever a stoppage occurred and bring the wire down to be repaired. Try how he would, and he tells us he tried very hard, he could not accomplish this feat. He was not an expert in athletics, and could always place more reliance on his brains than on his muscles.

As it happened, his climbing abilities were never put to the test, and he escaped the awful ordeal he had so much dreaded.

The way in which the young telegraph messenger gained his next promotion is in keeping with his whole career. Before the operators arrived in the morning, it was the custom of the telegraph boys to practise on the instruments by communicating with other boys along the lines. Young Carnegie took full advantage of this opportunity. He was by nature well equipped for the work, having a marvelous ear for sound and being wonderfully expert in distinguishing notes and tones. All the messages in those days were read, but young Andrew was quick to see the immense advantage of taking them by sound. Mr. J. D. Reed, in his " History of the Telegraph," referring to Andrew Carnegie at this time, says: "I liked the boy's looks, and it was very easy to see that though he was little he was full of spirit. He had not been with me a month when he began to ask whether I would teach him to telegraph. I began to instruct him, and found him an apt pupil. He spent all his spare time in practice, sending and receiving by sound, not by tape, as was -largely the custom in those days. Soon he could, do as well as myself.

It was not long ere an opportunity came for Andrew to use his knowledge. One morning while he was practicing a death message was signaled from Philadelphia. Death messages were considered of great importance, but the opening was too good to be lost, and confident in his powers Andrew attended to the call. When the operator arrived he found the message transcribed, and, moreover, it was perfectly correct. This clever piece of work brought young Andrew into notice, and proved for him the first stepping-stone to success. Shortly afterwards he was promoted to the position of an operator, with a salary of three hundred dollars a year.

He had long looked forward to the time when he should draw such a sum, for he had regarded it as the ideal standard of comfort. For a youth of sixteen it was indeed a promising start. This advance came at an opportune moment, for his father had recently died, and the burden of maintaining the home now fell chiefly upon his youthful shoulders.

The following incident illustrates the confidence reposed in him by those with whom he came in contact. Pittsburgh had a supply of six newspapers, and they all drew their information from the same telegraphic service. The copyist offered young Andrew a dollar a week if he would do the transcribing. The offer was accepted. He had always desired to see some of his own handiwork in the papers, and he liked to be brought in contact with the young fellows connected with the press. The extra dollar a week he thus earned he looked upon as "pure business," inasmuch as it represented a transaction entirely on his own account, and therefore he felt justified in retaining the remuneration for his own use. This was his first bit of capital

Everything young Carnegie was set to do he did with all his might, and there was no half-heartedness or indolence in his work.

Naturally such a diligent young man could not long remain unnoticed in a position which brought him into contact with the principal business men of the city. One of those who frequently visited the telegraph office was Mr. Thomas A. Scott, Superintendent of the Pittsburgh Division of the Pennsylvania Railroad.

Young Carnegie happened to be the operator through whom he sent most of his messages, and his keen eye singled him out as a young fellow of unusual promise. Accordingly, he spoke to him one day about his work, and offered him a situation as operator in the service of the railway company at an advance of ten dollars per month on the salary he was then receiving. Young Carnegie, knowing full well the kind of man who had made the offer, promptly accepted it.

He soon found that his new position gave him more scope for the development of his gifts and the exercise of his energies, and it was not long before he had made himself a favorite with his chief and won his confidence both as employer and friend.

One day Mr. Scott called Andrew aside and informed him that an excellent investment was open if he could obtain five hundred dollars. Owing to the death of the owner, there was an opportunity to acquire ten shares in the Adams Express Company. The shares were of the value of sixty dollars each, and Mr. Scott volunteered to advance one hundred dollars if Andrew could find the rest. The young operator knew it must be a genuine opportunity, as his chief had offered it, and his business instinct urged him to accept it. So he answered "Yes," though at the time he had no idea where the money was to be found. The door had been opened for a business investment, and immediate advantage must, he felt, be taken of the golden opportunity. The fact that the money was not ready for immediate handling did not deter him. He knew there was one member of the "family whose financial genius had surmounted many difficulties in the past, and he had abundant faith that she would devise some scheme for procuring the needful sum.

A family council was held the same evening, and when Andrew had explained all, his mother, ever on the lookout to help her industrious son, replied: "It must be done. We must mortgage the house. I will take the steamer in the morning for Ohio, and see uncle and ask him to arrange it." Her ability, pluck and resource triumphed. The visit proved successful, and the money was obtained. The shares were bought, and the little home mortgaged "to give our: boy a start."

Mr. Carnegie refers to this incident in glowing terms. His mother was the exalted ideal of his youth, and he says he can never adequately express what he owes to her constant love and wonderful business sagacity. "She succeeded. Where did she ever fail?" he once remarked.

It was her indefatigable energy, sound judgment and strong character which laid the comer-stone of his successful career. It is plainly evident that Andrew Carnegie inherited his genius for finance and his great commercial ability from his mother who little thought at the time that her boy would one day control millions, and have at his disposal more hard cash than any other living man.

This small transaction was destined to prove the forerunner of a long series of gigantic deals. All Mr. Carnegie's investments have yielded good returns, but this does not by any means signify that any young man who can borrow five hundred dollars will lay the basis of a great fortune, for, where one speculation succeeds, a hundred end in miserable heart-breaking failures. Mr. Carnegie was fortunate in making several lucrative investments, but his fortune has not been amassed by speculation, or gambling; it is the solid outcome of hard work, industrial genius and unflagging perseverance. He has never bought n or sold a share of stock on the Exchange.

The Adams Express Company paid monthly dividends of one per cent., and in due course the young investor received his first checque, which gave him boundless delight.

In his new position he took keen interest in his work; step by step he mastered every detail, and gradually acquired a comprehensive knowledge of the whole system. One morning Mr. Scott was late in arriving at the office, and in his absence an accident had occurred on one of the lines, and a very critical condition had arisen which needed prompt and decisive action. His knowledge enabled Carnegie to grasp the situation at once, and he took immediate action. There was only one track, and the freight trains were on the sidings along the line, waiting for the express, which had the right of way. He wired to the conductor of the express that he was going to give the freight trains three hours and forty minutes of his time, and asked for a reply. He then wired to the conductor of each freight train and started the whole of them. The telegrams were signed "Thomas A. Scott."

Mr. Scott thoroughly appreciated the ability displayed by his young lieutenant. He recognized that he could be depended upon at a crisis, and thenceforth regarded him as his right-hand man. Andrew was now Mr. Scott's private secretary, and gradually a strong affection arose between the railway chief and his protégé.

When the Civil War broke out Mr. Scott was made Assistant-Secretary of War. Andrew Carnegie had just entered his twenty-fourth year, and the position given him by his chief was a very responsible one. He had to see to the transport of the troops and stores, and generally to supervise the network of railways and telegraphs. The Confederates had already done considerable damage, but although the work was arduous he manfully stuck to his post, working indefatigably night and day. Precision of movement, promptness and punctuality in. the arrival and departure of the traffic, avoidance of muddle, and instant attention to stoppages and breakdowns - these things required a clear head and nerves of steel.

Curiously enough, although he did no actual fighting he was the third man wounded in the war. A telegraph wire which had been pinned to the ground, upon being loosened suddenly sprang up and cut a severe gash on his cheek, but he did not allow the injury to affect his duties. He was present at several battles, and at Bull Run was one of the last to leave the field. But it was at Washington, in the War Department, that he had his most interesting experiences, and it was while engaged in his duties there that he inaugurated a system of telegraphing by ciphers which was found to be of invaluable service.

The carnage, the bloodshed and the devastation of the land made so deep an impression upon his mind that he has ever since had a horror of war; in season and out of season he has been a strong advocate of peace, and the soldier's profession is one which he abhors.

He had no great liking for his duties, and was not sorry when his chief returned to Pittsburgh on June 1st, 1862

In an endeavor to discover the factors of Mr. Carnegie's success, one is struck by the succession of

THE CARNEGIE HOME AT DUNFERMLINE, SCOTLAND
The upper left-hand window marks the room in which Andrew Carnegie was born

opportunities that came to him for making money, and the insight with which on the one hand he estimated their true value, and the promptness with which on the other hand he took advantage of them. The element of chance in his investments was reduced to a minimum, and he only put his money into ventures with which he was practically acquainted. This fact was signally demonstrated by his next investment.

Shortly after his return from the war, while traveling on the railway, he was accosted by a strange gentleman who asked him if he was connected with the Pennsylvania Railroad Company. On hearing that this was so, the stranger drew from a bag he was carrying the model of a sleeping-car. Mr. Carnegie, in describing the incident, says: "He did not need to explain it at great length. I seemed to see its value in a flash. Railroad cars in which people could sleep on long journeys - of course there were no railroads across the continent yet - struck me as being the very thing for this land of magnificent distances. I told him I would speak about his model to Mr. Scott, and I did so enthusiastically." He went so far in its praise as to assert that it was "one of the inventions of the age." Mr. Scott saw the inventor, and the outcome of the negotiations was that two trial cars were run over the Pennsylvania Railroad. They proved an encouraging success, and it was decided to form a sleeping-car company. Mr. Carnegie was offered an interest, which he willingly accepted.

As on the last occasion, so on this, he was faced with the difficulty of providing the necessary funds, which in this instance amounted to two hundred and twenty dollars. He applied to his bank, and it was a delightful surprise to him when the manager, patting him on the back, said, "You are all right, Andy," and willingly discounted his note. Mr. Carnegie, referring to this incident, remarks, "It is a proud day for a man when he pays his last note, but not to be named in comparison with the day in which he makes his first one, and gets a banker to accept it. I have tried both and know." The investment proved a lucrative one, and Mr. Carnegie was enabled to pay the subsequent calls on his stock out of the dividends distributed. The company was eventually absorbed by the Pullman Palace Car Company.

This transaction put Mr. Carnegie in possession of his first substantial sum of capital. Shortly afterwards he received his last promotion as an employee by his appointment to be superintendent of the Pittsburgh Division of the Pennsylvania Railroad.

Andrew Carnegie

CHAPTER III

FORTUNE'S FLOOD

THE results accruing from his investment in the Woodruff Sleeping Car Company, added to his weekly savings, placed Mr. Carnegie in possession of a fair sum of money. He had repaid all the loans received from his mother and his banker, and was now free to make what use he thought best of his moderate capital; nor had he long to wait before an opening was afforded for this. Andrew Carnegie "struck oil," and struck it to some purpose. Prom that profitable source he extracted a return that far exceeded his utmost expectations. He got in almost at the beginning of the mineral oil boom, when the vast possibilities of the industry were little understood, and the great utility of the product had not been discovered. In conjunction with some friends, he subscribed toward the purchase of the now famous Storey Farm, on Oil Creek, which was bought for the sum of forty thousand dollars. At that time the oil was running into a creek where lay some flat-bottomed scows which were fitted up for its conveyance. Upon a certain day each week the creek was flooded by means of a temporary dam, and these scows were floated down to the Alleghany River. The well was then producing one hundred barrels daily, but Mr. Carnegie doubted if this output could be maintained. It was therefore decided to store up a large reserve, which it was hoped would command a high price in the time of expected scarcity. For this purpose a reservoir was made with a capacity of 100,000 barrels, or 3,300,000 gallons. This was filled, and its contents were valued at $1,000,000, but as the reservoir leaked very badly and large losses occurred through evaporation oil was still allowed to run into it. Time went on, thousands of barrels were sold, but still to the surprise of the proprietors the supply seemed as plentiful as ever, and at last some idea of the extent of the real resources of their property dawned upon them. The well, or rather the shares in it, reached a value on the Stock Exchange of $5,000,000, and in one year the syndicate paid the handsome sum of $1,000,000 in cash dividends - certainly an astonishing return on an investment of $40,000.

When he joined in this oil venture Mr. Carnegie was twenty-seven years of age, but though oil has made more than one millionaire, it was not destined to be the means by which he was to amass his fortune. Leaving the oil springs to his contemporary, Mr. Rockefeller, he turned his energies in another direction. He had not long been in his new position of Superintendent on the Pittsburgh Division of the Pennsylvania Railroad, when the company began to make some experiments with an iron bridge. Up to this time bridges had been made of wood, and the Pennsylvania Railroad was the first to give a trial to another material. The experiment was completely successful, and gave rise to much thought in the mind of Mr. Carnegie. There had been so many delays on the railways through bridges being burned or broken, that he had long ago come to the conclusion that cast iron or some other tough noninflammable material would have to displace wood in their construction; and after thoroughly considering the matter, he came to the conclusion that there was a great opening for a firm that could manufacture the parts for iron bridges.

As usual, he had no sooner convinced himself that the idea was sound and promising, than he commenced to look around for ways and means to put his plans into operation. No time was to be lost. The future steel manufacturer was fully alive to the truth embodied in Shakespeare's famous lines -

"There is a tide in the affairs of men
Which, taken at the flood, leads on to fortune."

He formed another syndicate and started the Keystone Bridge Works. The first large piece of work done by the firm was to build the great bridge over the Ohio River, which has a span of three hundred feet. As Mr. Carnegie had foreseen, the substitution of iron for wood became general, both in bridge building and in many other directions, and the Keystone Company had soon largely to extend its works for increased production. Thus was laid the foundation of what are today the finest iron and steel works in the world

For many years Mr. Carnegie had aspired to enter business on his own account, and to be the employer of thousands of work-people; and when he felt satisfied that the prosperity of the new company was assured, he resigned his post with the Pennsylvania Railroad Company, in whose service he had risen from telegraph operator to divisional superintendent. Having relinquished his official duties, he was free to concentrate all his energy and genius on the development of his own business, and give full play to his marvelous powers of organization. Gradually the superior merits of iron bridges became widely known. The Keystone Company were the first in the field, and as they enjoyed an excellent reputation for first-class workmanship and prompt delivery, they soon reaped a rich harvest. Orders flowed in from all quarters, and the increase of business has continued without a break right up to the present time.

The success of the Keystone Bridge Works was achieved through the most progressive business methods and by the boldest and most enterprising innovations. Mr. Carnegie has always been a man of great commercial daring, although no one could charge him with recklessness, for all his ventures have been preceded by thorough examination, and consideration of the prospects of success. Once having convinced himself of the value of an innovation or the soundness of a scheme, he never wavered in his purpose, but, confident in his ability, and encouraged by past successes, set himself to carry his enterprises through to a triumphant issue. Calling to his aid every force that could help him in any way, and perfecting his organization at every point, he was prompt to avail himself of the discoveries of science. His works have always been equipped with the most up-to-date machinery, while he has met the large and continuous increase of business with correspondingly large extensions of his works. All this was accomplished only by the most resolute determination, for he had constant difficulties to contend with. His credit, however, was good. He had succeeded so far with everything he had undertaken, and this fact aided him in overcoming the greatest obstacle to his progress, namely, the raising of capital.

Mr. Carnegie's next great effort, and the one that lifted him into the position of the foremost iron and steel producer in the world, was prompted by a discovery which he made when on a visit to England. This was in the year 1868, just at the time when the Bessemer invention had emerged from the experimental stage into an accepted workable process of incalculable value to the industrial world. Mr. Carnegie, of course, had his hand on it in an instant. He learned that in many directions, especially in rails, iron was rapidly being displaced by the steel produced by this new process. To a large iron founder this was a matter of vital importance. The necessity for substituting steel for iron in the manufacture of rails had been recognized for some time by railway experts. Mr. Carnegie himself, when in the service of the Pennsylvania Railroad Company, had suggested a process for hardening iron rails by carbon, precisely the same as the Harvey process. The company spent $20,000 on the experiment, which was attended with excellent results, for the rails turned out were a great improvement on the old ones, and gave great satisfaction. But the steel rails produced by the Bessemer process were an altogether superior product, and Mr. Carnegie recognized that he must at once adopt that process in his works. Accordingly he acquired all the necessary knowledge and equipment, and immediately returned to America to commence operations by the erection of an enormous plant for the Bessemer process of steel manufacture. As he had been practically the first in America to recognize the immense superiority of iron over wood for certain purposes, so now he was the first to realize the great superiority of steel over iron. Just as he had reaped a rich harvest through his foresight in being ready to turn out iron bridges, so now he reaped an even richer harvest in being prepared to supply the sudden demand for steel rails.

In mentioning England as the source from whence this "Steel King" drew his inspiration to launch out in the direction of steel production, one cannot help being struck with the keen irony of the circumstance in the light of present day competition. At this time America had not the slightest chance in competition with Britain for the markets of the world, and thousands of tons of iron and steel were exported to the United States by Britain despite the high tariff duties. Mr. Carnegie had little hope that America could compete with England in neutral markets, and none that she could eclipse her. Writing in 1883, he expressed the following opinion: "America can only render herself ridiculous by entering the water. That is England's domain. The first cost of a steel ship is about one-half on the Clyde what it is on the Delaware. Steel can be made, and is made, in Great Britain for one-half of its cost here. Not in our day will it be wise for America to leave the land. It is a very fair division as it stands - the land for America, the sea for England." Nineteen years later, while Mr. Carnegie is still expecting a long lease of life, Mr. J. Pierpont Morgan has surprised England and the world at large by acquiring for American interests a mercantile marine of great ships of several lines. Mr. Carnegie's remarks in 1883 show how utterly in the dark even the most far-seeing of America's industrial leaders were regarding the vast potentialities of their country.

The developments brought about by this introduction of the Bessemer steel process were so promising that Mr. Carnegie found himself face to face with a remarkable situation. He had now reached the supreme crisis in his career. Whatever course he decided to adopt, either that of resting on his oars or of pressing forward to further progress, was almost certain to bring him great wealth. He elected to advance and extend. The next step he took was destined to revolutionize the industrial methods of the world, and to put him on the road to the acquirement of such a fortune as would astonish mankind. A new era in industrial history was at hand, and why should he not head the advance!

A close study of the position convinced him that no country in the world could better take advantage of the Bessemer process than the United States, with its vast undeveloped mineral resources and its phenomenal industrial growth. He drew up a scheme as comprehensive as it was daring. This involved nothing less than the erection of more great works and the acquisition of his own coal and iron fields and of his own transport facilities. It shows the indomitable spirit of the man, and the intensity of his ambition, that although already the possessor of a fortune, he should risk all in grappling with such a mighty venture as this. Never before had he shown such energy and determination. Neither money nor labor was spared in the building of the vast premises now called the Edgar Thompson Steel Works, across the Monongahela River from Homestead. The most skilled engineers available were employed in equipping the works with the finest plant money could buy; and to supplement this he acquired vast tracts of land containing immeasurable mineral resources. He had to go from 700 to 900 miles away, to the shores of the Great Lakes, in order to procure the bulk of his properties. He followed this up by purchasing a fleet of steamers to transport the ore across the Great Lakes; and by building his own railway of about 425 miles to carry it down to his works round Pittsburgh.

All the world knows how splendidly this courageous enterprise was rewarded. The superiority of steel rails over those made from iron was speedily acknowledged, and Mr. Carnegie was simply overwhelmed with orders. Vast as his output was, it was totally inadequate to meet the demand. What he had thought were ample preparations turned out to be altogether insufficient. He was now determined to become the undisputed master of the steel market, and to shrink from no responsibility in order to maintain his lead. It was imperative that he should largely, increase his productive capacity. He had to "strike while the iron was hot" and could not wait for the erection of fresh works. He therefore turned his attention to the premises of a rival concern, The Homestead Steel Company, whose enormous foundries were close to his own works, and opened up negotiations with these competitors which resulted in their absorption by the Carnegie combination. Further extensions and acquisitions were made until, in 1888, Mr. Carnegie possessed no less than seven great iron and steel works, besides his vast coal fields, iron mines, railways, docks and fleets of steamers.

Two hundred and fifty million dollars is a stupendous sum, but when one considers the unique position Mr. Carnegie obtained in the greatest industry in the world, it is not surprising that he succeeded in amassing even such a colossal fortune. He appeared with his magnificent manufacturing facilities just at the period when the prosperity of America was in its infancy. The unparalleled railway extension in the country had scarcely commenced; great towns were springing up on all sides, and in every direction enormous quantities of iron and steel were needed for structural purposes. He had reduced the cost of production to a minimum. By means of his railway and steamboat services he had brought his mineral resources within easy access of his foundries, and had acquired every tool and process necessary to manipulate with his own materials, and by, his own workmen the rough ore into the finished product. He was thus well able to defy competition from any quarter, and having secured the home trade, he stepped forward to invade the markets of the world. He extended his trade on all sides; but vast as his volume of business was, and rapid as his progress had been, he was able, through his wonderful organization, to keep his business thoroughly under control, so that his profits leaped ahead at a corresponding rate. It was a glorious triumph for skilful organization and enterprise.

It is difficult to realize the full extent of this mighty achievement and the influence it has exerted on the progress of the world. No one can deny such a man a tribute of the highest admiration. He is a genius in the most exact sense of the word, and he has used his gifts and powers to stimulate to a remarkable degree the forward march of civilization. Mr. Carnegie takes his place among those giants of humanity who, by the heights of their attainments, have lifted to a higher plane the possibilities of man, and have forced a point upward the human standard of excellence, from which succeeding generations will start forward to further progress.

CHAPTER IV

THE STEEL MASTER

MR. CARNEGIE, as the undisputed monarch of iron and steel, towered head and shoulders above all his rivals. He was the chief of a trade combination that enjoyed the distinction of being the largest employer of labor in the world. The Carnegie Steel Company, which was reconstructed at the beginning of 1900 with a capital of $100,000,000, owned three immense works - the Homestead, the Edgar Thompson and the Duquesne, and seven smaller ones. When in full swing it is estimated that this huge concern gave employment to no less than 45000 work-people, and if we reckon the small average of five members to a family it means that this one firm controlled the happiness of over 225,000 persons. The works at Homestead alone covered seventy-five acres of land and employed nearly 4,000 men. One who has visited these works says: "On first viewing Homestead two thoughts are forced upon a mmd of mechanical bent, namely, the vast wealth necessary to build, equip and run a plant of such magnitude; and the ingenuity and skill required to devise and manage it." The works were managed by experienced men of great ability, and the workmen were a highly skilled body second to none in the country. It was Mr. Carnegie's habit to have mailed to him, whatever part of the world he might be, a tabulated form ingeniously devised, containing the details of the total product for the day of each and every department of the business. In this way he was able to keep in constant touch with the affairs of the firm. Every Monday a meeting of the members of the firm was held, all important matters were discussed and decided upon there, and full minutes of each meeting were regularly sent to any absent member. As Mr. Carnegie lived in New York, this plan kept him well informed on all plans of action.

The Homestead mill manufactured armor plates for the ships for the navy and all kinds of structural material. It contained twenty open-hearth furnaces and two ten-ton Bessemer converters having a daily product of 3,000 tons of steel ingots, which were used in the manufacture of a great variety of articles, from the steel rims of a bicycle to the 200-ton armor plates of a battleship. Here also were constructed the gigantic steel frames for many buildings, and particularly for "sky-scrapers." In the manufacturing processes electricity plays an important part. This valuable force was used as the motive-power for moving huge blocks of material and in a hundred and one other ways. Masses weighing two hundred tons and more were handled with ease by the electric machines, all of which were fed from a single station, whence wires extended, like the arteries in the human body, to the different departments. The workmen became accustomed to the use of the electric agent and handled it as confidently as they would steam or water. In every respect the machinery was of the most modem description, and was supplemented in every possible manner by the latest devices of scientific discovery.

Next in importance to the Homestead were the Edgar Thompson Steel Works, situated on the other side of the river. These were chiefly devoted to the production of pig-iron and the manufacture of steel rails. The furnaces had a daily output of 2,800 tons of pig-iron, a large part of which was used on the premises, and the remainder transferred to Homestead. The rail mill was perhaps the finest in the world, and was capable of producing 1,600 tons of steel rails per day. The third large foundry, the Duquense, on the Monongahela River, had furnaces that produced in one day as much as the largest furnaces thirty years ago produced in a week. They had a capacity for daily converting 2,000 tons of pig-iron into billets, rails, sheets, bars, etc.

In addition to these vast works under Mr. Carnegie's control, there were the wire and nail mills at Beaver Falls; the structural works at Pittsburgh; the Isabella furnaces ; the Lucy furnaces; and the Keystone Bridge Works. Another branch of the Carnegie combination was the Frick Coke Company, which was the largest of its kind in the world. It owned coal-bearing lands to the extent of 40,000 acres, and in addition possessed more than two-thirds of the famous Connellsville coalfields. It had an operating plant consisting of 10,500 ovens with a possible daily output of 20,000 tons. Every day a line of railway trucks five miles long conveyed the product to the various foundries of the firm.* The Carnegie combination also owned vast tracts of land, including the richest iron ore mines on Lake Superior. It possessed a special fleet of steamers for the transport of the ore from the mines on Lake Superior to Cleveland on Lake Erie, a distance of over 700 miles, and had laid its own private railway to take the ore from Cleveland down to its various works round Pittsburgh. The company possessed a large extent of natural gas bearing land, from which the gas was conveyed in pipes to the furnaces. It had a private telegraph system, and its wires ran to all the important industrial centres of the country. Branch offices of the firm were to be found in all the large cities of America, and its total clerical staff was so numerous that at the head office,

Pittsburgh, a hundred and fifty clerks could take a vacation at one time without causing any disorganization of the system.

* These figures were compiled some years ago. The productions of all the Carnegie properties have largely increased since.

The plant of the Carnegie works was capable of producing an annual output in steel alone of 3,000,000 tons, of which about two-thirds would be open-hearth steel. This Titanic concern was held together by the most perfect organization, in which the highest degree of skill was employed.

Here are a few facts to illustrate the wonderful administration of this vast industry. It was possible to transport ore from the shores of Lake Superior to Pittsburgh, nearly a thousand miles away, and convert it into steel in ten days, despite the fact that three separate shipments have to be made! Some of the open mines at Lake Superior were capable of special treatment, and for digging the ore in these steam shovels were used. One of these shovels could load a 2 5 -ton car in two and one-half minutes. The shovel picked up five tons of earth at every stroke, and filled the car in five operations.

At Duluth, the western head of Lake Superior, there were two loading jetties, each 2,000 feet long, and rows of ore bins built into these, each holding from 150 to 170 tons. The railroad ran over these bins, and dropped down their loads of twenty-five tons, to be subsequently shot into the holds of the ships. At these docks ore was shipped at the rate of 1,000 to 1,600 tons per vessel per hour. A 6,000-ton vessel, equal to the capacity of 750 8-ton cars, could be loaded with ore in six hours or less. Prom the Lake Superior district 17,000,000 tons were shipped in 1899. The railway traffic from the ore-receiving ports to the smelting furnaces, in some cases extending to 700 miles, was carried on by mammoth locomotives, some weighing 127 tons each, hauling 1,600 tons of ore in thirty cars - great steel trucks specially built to carry about fifty tons a piece.

At the mills the blast-furnaces were served by a hoisting engine controlled by a single individual. Here also the Wellman-Seaver electrical charging machines were used. This is the latest mechanical triumph of its kind, relieving human sinew and muscle of the strain and tension of heavy work amid the terrible heat of the smelting furnaces. It traveled on rails past the rows of furnaces, and the attendant, comfortably seated, merely moved an electrical switch which actuated a powerful arm of steel. This took charge of pig-iron, scrap and ore, which it deposited inside the furnaces. The machine fed furnace after furnace with their requirements of half a ton at a time in a few seconds each. The doors of the furnaces were opened and closed by water power. And so one might continue to enumerate the vast resources and the wonderful armory of this industrial king.

Such a magnificent aggregation of industrial power has never before been under the dominion of a single man. This vast organization, with its army of skilled workmen, was the great stumbling-block to the promoters when they first schemed to create a Steel Trust of such magnitude as would enable them to dominate the markets of the world. The properties under Mr. Carnegie's control were too great and the value of them too fully realized to allow of easy adjustment of ownership. The amounts offered Mr. Carnegie by the Trust organizers were entirely out of proportion to the value of the property and the negotiations fell through for the time.

Mr. Carnegie announced his intention of equipping enormous works at Conneaut, Ohio, at a cost of $15,000,000, to be devoted to special competition with the products of the Trust. He also decided to build up another steel mill which should surpass in capacity anything in existence. As for the Trust's control of the railways, he boldly declared that he would construct his own services.

This mood, characteristic of the man, showed more clearly than anything else could his confidence in his properties, and brought out in strong relief the value of the steel plants. The absolute necessity became evident that they must be included in the combination, and an offer was made Mr. Carnegie for his interests which, though so great as to be almost inconceivable, is believed to be in proper proportion to their value. Mr. Carnegie sold out on his own terms. He received for his interest $250,000,000 of bonds on the Trust's properties, bearing interest at the rate of five per cent, per annum.

In an address to the people of Pittsburgh, Mr. Carnegie explained the reasons that had prompted him to retire from business, as follows: "An opportunity to retire from business came to me unsought, which I considered it my duty to accept. My resolve was made in youth to retire before old age. From what I have seen around me, I cannot doubt the wisdom of this course, although the change is great, even serious, and seldom brings the happiness expected. But this is because so many, having abundance to retire upon, have so little to retire to. I have always felt that old age should be spent, not as the Scotch say, in 'makin' mickle mair,' but in making a good use of what has been acquired, and I hope my friends at Pittsburgh will approve of my action in retiring while still in full health and vigor, and I can reasonably expect many years for usefulness in fields which have other than personal aims."

It must not be understood for one moment that Mr. Carnegie's opposition to the Trust was actuated in the slightest degree by any personal objection to the formation of these mammoth undertakings. The J Carnegie Company, of which he was the head, was in its way a huge combination; and on many occasions he has expressed the opinion that trusts are a great benefit to the community, and are simply a result of the advance of human enterprise.

So late as May, 1901, he said: "All these consolidations of steel trusts, railways and steamship lines are steps in advance of still greater movements which will distinguish the twentieth century. This unification of transport by sea and land is a mark of genuine world-progress. Hereafter American railway lines will be under one interest from the Atlantic to the Pacific, and one management in New York will be able to fix rates to meet the situation. In a short time the great trunk railways will own steamship lines on the Pacific and Atlantic, thus consolidating transport on land and sea, and the business of the world will be carried on with but little division. It would be unwise not to promote these movements."

There is much shrewd common sense in these remarks, but the growth of these gigantic combinations has been so rapid that widespread suspicion exists as to their soundness. If their main object is to be to gain a monopoly, then they deserve to fail, for monopolies are often an industrial evil both to the work-people and to the community at large.

In surveying the phenomenal success of Mr. Carnegie, one's curiosity is aroused as to the instruments he employed to attain it and the means by which he exercised control over his extensive interests. The most important factor has undoubtedly been his consummate genius for organization, and almost on a par with this must be placed his remarkable insight into human nature. Mr. Carnegie himself attributes his success chiefly to the band of clever young men which he gathered round him. He has an unbounded belief in young men, and he has never been afraid to intrust them with the most important duties. "It is astonishing," he says, "what a young man can do if he is only trusted." His method has been to keep a keen lookout for any young fellows of exceptional ability, whether in his own employ or in the employ of others. And rarely did his judgment fail him. Scores of wealthy men in America to-day owe their position to Andrew Carnegie's timely encouragement.

Mr. H. C. Prick, one of the foremost men in the commercial world to-day, is one of those whom Mr. Carnegie credited with the making of a first-class business man, and he took him from the employ of another firm and gave him a position in his own organization. Another instance is that of a young fellow who served behind a shop counter in Dunfermline. He sent him to Pittsburgh and gave him the usual opportunities to distinguish himself. The young man rose rapidly, was finally admitted into partnership, and is now a rich man. Perhaps the most striking tribute to Mr. Carnegie's perceptive faculty is Mr. Schwab, who is now receiving an enormous salary as manager of the new steel trust, the United States Steel Corporation. He entered Mr. Carnegie's service as a boy, and by his extraordinary smartness and his rare capacity for work he attracted the attention of his employer. He had neither capital nor influence, but he had merit, and he steadily advanced, each new promotion revealing in him greater ability, until he attained the highest position in the greatest industrial concern and was president of the company before he reached thirty. These are the men who formed Mr. Carnegie's working cabinet.

It is hard to define in exact terms the power which Mr. Carnegie had of stimulating his subordinates and infusing them with his own consuming enthusiasm. He had a perfect genius for discovering young men of exceptional ability, and, having secured them, they were given a fair chance to prove their worth. No favoritism of any kind was allowed, all promotion being solely by merit. His first partner, David A. Stewart, and his brother, Tom Carnegie, both had grown-up sons, but none of these young men were admitted to the concern, and at death their parents' interests were paid out. "Dead heads" were a luxury never tolerated in the Carnegie Company. Having worked his own way in the world, Mr. Carnegie knew how best to encourage a deserving youth. "Responsibility," he once said, "thrown upon a young man that is the thing to bring out what is in him." But he insisted that the youth himself should be thoroughly interested in his work, and be animated with a strong desire to succeed. "Concentration" he says, "is my motto - first honesty, then industry, then concentration," and he expected it to be the motto of his employees. If they did not give their whole energies to their work they lost their places or were degraded. Each new man had to maintain the standard of excellence reached by his predecessor. Mere mediocrity and languid interest were not tolerated.

On the other hand, hard and conscientious work was promptly and handsomely rewarded, and when a subordinate was appointed to the position of a manager, Mr. Carnegie maintained that the test of his ability was not what he did himself, but what he could get others to do in cooperation with him. "The great manager," he said, "is the man who knows how to surround himself with men much abler than himself. I have always found that a manager of one of our great works has been able to make excellent managers out of material which before his magic touch was quite mediocre. He inspires his subordinates to almost superhuman efforts."

It was men of this caliber that were given a stake in the business in the shape of stock, or who were promoted to be partners. They worked together, heart and soul, for a common interest, and Mr. Carnegie is proud of the fact that he has never had occasion to exercise his authority over any one of them. He pays to these talented, ambitious young fellows an unqualified tribute of admiration -

"I do not believe any one man can make a success of a business nowadays. I am sure I never could have done so without my partners, of whom I had thirty-two, the brightest and cleverest young fellows in the world. All are equal to each other, as the members of the Cabinet are equal. The chief must only be first among equals. I know that every one of my partners would have smiled at the idea of my being his superior, although the principal stockholder. The way they differed from me and beat me many a time was delightful to behold. I never enjoyed anything more than to get a sound thrashing in an argument at the hands of these young geniuses. No man will make a great business who wants to do it all himself or to get all the credit for doing it. I believe firmly in youths as executive agents. Older heads should be reserved for counsel."

An English writer has called attention to this and says that "Mr. Carnegie sets an example that British employers might well take note of. There can be no doubt that to this practice of placing young men in responsible positions is largely due the enterprise and progress of American commerce."

The power of organization and the faculty of recognizing and developing dependable assistants contributed largely to Mr. Carnegie's success.

CHAPTER V

AS AN EMPLOYER OF LABOR

OPINION regarding Mr. Carnegie as an employer of labor is sharply divided. On the one hand he is looked upon as a man who has violated in practice all the excellent theory that he has written on the subject; and, on the other hand, it is asserted that he has done everything possible for his work-people compatible with the maintenance of his business in the face of fierce competition.

In attempting to review Mr. Carnegie's record in this respect, it is of the first importance to take into consideration the conditions of capital and labor that existed in the United States during his career. The policy of an employer in America and the policy of an employer in England must be judged from different standpoints, for the two are on a totally different footing with their employees and have to contend with an entirely diverse environment. In America, even at the present time, employers and employees are often at variance, and during Mr. Carnegie's time, ten to twenty years ago, the period with which we are concerned, the antagonism between the two was much more intense than it is to-day.

The set purpose of the employers naturally was to extract from their workmen the maximum of labor at the minimum of cost, both in wages and accommodation. The avowed object of the workmen was to obtain the highest wages and the shortest hours possible, and to work no harder than was necessary. Each party was aware of the intentions of the other, and consequently each watched every move of the other keenly. Wrecking tactics by the one side at the time strikes were in progress were followed by swift punishment. But in the main the weakest had gone to the wall, and the workman was under the heel of his employer, though occasionally, being supported by public opinion, the workman won.

Such a state of distrust between capital and labor could only be regarded as deplorable in the extreme by a man of the temperament of Mr. Carnegie, who has always been astute enough to recognize that good feeling between master and workman is essential for the highest prosperity of both. He considers that nothing pays so well in business as generous treatment and mutual good-will. His experience, he says, goes to prove that the firm which has a reputation for taking the best care of its men has the best chance, because the best men will gravitate to that firm and stay with it. Mr. Carnegie's prime prescription for smooth working in the industrial arena is the copartnership principle, but as that was not practicable he advocated the next best thing, namely, the sliding-scale arrangement of remuneration. This part of his theory he put into practice in his own works. The scale there was based on the price of the product. Once a month a committee approved by the men met, and before this committee was laid all the information necessary to enable it to estimate what prices the firm would obtain. An average price was then agreed upon, and this formed the basis for the wages for the ensuing month.

Of course, the weakness of this system is that, as circumstances change, differences arise regarding the fairness of the percentage of remuneration on the price of the products, and in this respect it is little better than the old method. Its great advantage lies in the fact that it brings masters and men into contact and tends to promote mutual self-respect. Whenever they do come together on such occasions, Mr. Carnegie holds that the employer, being the better trained and more cultured party, should exercise great forbearance in regard to the men's behavior. If they are rough and surly in their manners, and at times somewhat arrogant in their bearing, he should overlook this as the outcome of their inferior education and mode of life. He also thinks that it is not too much to expect men entrusted with the management of great properties to devote some part of their time to searching out any causes of discontent among their employees, and, having satisfied themselves that they are genuine, to meet the men more than half-way in an endeavor to settle them.

But he insisted on the men doing their best. They must work and work hard. He tolerates no slackness. Idlers are an abomination to him. He is convinced that a state of regular labor is the best possible condition for the human race, and produces the best citizen. He honors the laborer far above the aristocrat. "The lot of a skilled workman," he says," is far better than that of the heir to an hereditary title, who is very likely to lead an unhappy, wicked life." Mr. Carnegie was once asked his views on the "too old at forty" problem. He replied: "A man at forty who is in search of something to do has a prima facie case against him. Long before he is forty he should have shown himself to be indispensable and received either a high salary or an interest in the business. Of course, there are exceptional cases where a worthy man is suddenly deprived of work at forty. His is a sad case indeed." He does not advise workmen in comfortable circumstances to emigrate and take great risks. If a man can make thirty shillings a week in his native land, Mr. Carnegie thinks he would be very foolish to leave it, unless he is impelled by an uncontrollable ambition and has no ties to bind him. Even though men may be fortunate enough to earn higher wages, very likely the conditions of life will not suit them and they will become dissatisfied. "Look before you leap" is the advice he offers.

Thus far we have studied Mr. Carnegie in theory now let us see how he has put all these admirable sentiments and unimpeachable principles into practice. The best test that can be applied is the condition of labor surrounding his own workmen. Mr. Hamlin Garland, a well-known writer, though having no technical experience, describes the impressions he received from a visit to the Homestead works. His training as a novelist naturally impelled him to look at things from the descriptive writer's point of view, and not become interested in the picturesque, both horrible and attractive. In his approach to Homestead Mr. Garland was struck by the desolate appearance of the district, and the wretchedness of the town itself, he says, was deplorable. "The streets were horrible; the buildings were poor; the sidewalks were sunken and full of holes; and the crossings were formed of sharp-edged stones like rocks in a river bed. Everywhere the yellow mud of the streets lay kneaded into sticky masses, through which groups of pale, lean men slouched in faded garments, grimy with the soot and dirt of the mills. The town was as squalid as could well be imagined, and the people were mainly of the discouraged and sullen type to be found everywhere where labor passes into the brutalizing stage of severity."

These depressing conditions are apparently inseparable from a newly established iron or steel mill in any locality, and this is especially true where soft coal is used. Grime, heat, hard, exhausting labor, these are conditions that are to be found in every steel mill, and the works of the Carnegie Company differed little from other manufactories of the same kind except in extent, but it may be truly said that the larger the mill the more depressing the conditions.

After commenting on the muggy, smoke-laden atmosphere, he proceeds to describe the conditions inside the mills, and the men engaged at their tasks, and tells us that they worked with a sort of desperate attention and alertness.

"That looks like hard work," I said to one of them to whom my companion introduced me. He was breathing hard from his labor.

"Hard! I guess it's hard. I lost forty pounds the first three months I came into the business. It sweats the life out of a man. I often drink two buckets of water in twelve hours; the sweat drips through my sleeves, and runs down my legs and fills my shoes."

"But that isn't the worst of it," said my guide, a former employee. "It's a dog's life. Now those men work twelve hours, and sleep and eat out ten more. You can see a man don't have much time for anything else. You can't see your friends or do anything but work. That's why I got out of it. I used to come home so exhausted, staggering like a man with a 'jag.'"

Again and again he is impressed with the general appearance of exhaustion that is shown in the haggard faces of the toilers, and he says "their work is of the sort that hardens and coarsens." Everywhere in the enormous sheds were pits gaping like the mouth of hell, and ovens emitting a terrible degree of heat, with grimy men filling and lining them. One man jumps down, works desperately for a few minutes, and is then pulled up, exhausted. Another immediately takes his place; there is no hesitation. When he spoke to the men they laughed. It was winter when he made his visit. They told him to come in the summer, during July, when one could scarcely breathe. An old workman, relating the experience of his first day's toil, says he applied for work, and the superintendent, saying he looked strong and tough, set him on the pit work. For the first time in his life he fainted repeatedly, and when he left at night he could scarcely drag himself home.

They take great risks, too; and the injuries sustained are of a most frightful character. An explosion in the pouring of the molten metal, and half a dozen men are terribly mangled and one or two killed. Such incidents are not infrequent. The continuous dread of an accident, combined with the intense drive of the work, constitute a fearful strain. This is a fearful picture, painted in the darkest, most repulsive colors, but this is but one side of it. Nothing is said of the comfortable homes which steady employment at from four to ten dollars a day enabled the steady sober workman to maintain - the self-confidence that continuous employment begets. The environments of the mills were improved as rapidly as possible, streets were paved, schools were established, and public institutions of various kinds were initiated. Several free educational institutions were founded by Mr. Carnegie in an attempt to help his workmen help themselves. The other side of this picture is full of light and hope, though there are many exceptions. Many of the men have happy families, and those of the better class are very well off. The company houses are very good, and have all modem conveniences, and the men who are sober and care for their families, besides being prosperous live comfortably.

The effect of the work on these men was brought out in a conversation with one of them which Mr. Garland had the morning after his visit to the mills. "The worst part of the whole business," said the workman, "is, it brutalizes a man. You can't help it. You start to be a man, but you become more and more a machine, and pleasures are few and far between. It's like any severe labor; it drags you down mentally and morally just as it does physically. I wouldn't mind it so much but for the long hours. Twelve hours is too long."

The rate of pay in the works varied with the class of labor. But, speaking generally, at Homestead the workmen received a daily wage of from $1.50 to $10.00. The old experienced men in these works are hardened specimens of humanity, with muscles and bodies as tough as the steel they handle. They are wonderfully deft and skillful, and are capable of turning out an immense amount of work at a high rate of speed.

Mr. Carnegie freely admits that English workmen would not work as these men do, and he calculates that each man does nearly twice as much as his English prototype. He considers the climate of America much more invigorating than that of Britain, and he puts forward other contributory causes of the difference.

But there can be no doubt that the extra work is forced by the tremendous drive or pressure of the American system. The men are bent upon earning high wages, and the masters are determined to beat all competition. Progress, the accumulation of wealth, complete supremacy over all competitors, these are the paramount considerations, and everything less is disregarded.

What reply does Mr. Carnegie or any other employer make when easier conditions are suggested? He tells you that it is impossible unless all manufacturers in the same line agree on practically the same conditions: competition is inexorable. If these measures were not adopted, they would be left behind in the fighter. And Mr. Carnegie is certainly not the man to be "left"; rather is he the man to leave others. He is a typical American employer. Nowhere has the drive and strain been more intense, and the discipline more rigorous and unbending, than in the works of the Carnegie Company. But if Mr. Carnegie drives his men hard, he pays them well. He claims that the wages paid in his works have been from ten to fifteen per cent, higher than in any other works of a similar nature in the United

States. Inside his works he was in that respect superior to the typical American employer, and outside he is far ahead of his commercial brethren. The average manufacturer in America, it is said, compares very unfavorably with his British rival in the interest he takes in the well-being of his work-people during their leisure time. Homestead, as we have seen, was a dismal place. Model working-class communities were conspicuous by their absence.

Mr. Carnegie, we know, has done and is doing a great deal in the way of providing libraries, music halls and clubs, and he has recently made a gift of $4,000,000 for the formation of a pension fund for his work-people. In another way Mr. Carnegie has shown his breadth of sympathy. On the principle of helping those who help themselves, the Carnegie firm allows every workman to deposit his savings in the business and pays him six per cent, interest on the money invested. On the other hand, the firm is willing to lend to any of its workmen desirous of building or purchasing a house the sum needed for the purpose, charging interest at the rate of six per cent, on the loan.

Mr. Carnegie is also deserving of the highest praise for the strenuous efforts he has made to reduce the hours of labor in America by working the eight-hour instead of the twelve-hour shifts. His action in this matter convincingly proves his real desire to alleviate the exceptional strain to which American people are subject. He says: "I sympathize with the desire to have shorter hours of labor. We have too long hours of labor in America. There is not a blast-furnace or manufactory that has to run night and day at which the workers do not work twelve hours a day, the twenty-four hours being divided into two shifts. But to reduce the hours of labor in works that have to run night and day can only be done by a general law compelling all such works to adopt eight-hour shifts. We tried this voluntarily ourselves at Pittsburgh for two years. We worked all the blast-furnace men on three shifts of eight hours each, hoping that other iron manufacturers would be induced or compelled to follow our example. But only one firm in the whole country did so; and finally competition became so keen that we were forced to go back to the twelve-hour shifts. It was a question whether we were to run the works at a loss or not, and after losing at least $500,000 by the experiment, we had to ask our men to return to the two shifts a day. We offered to divide with the men the extra cost of thirty-three and one-third per cent, which the three shifts involved, so that we might continue the eight-hour system, the firm paying seventeen per cent, and the men sixteen per cent; but rather than do this they decided to go back to the two shifts of twelve hours a day."

These facts should be carefully considered by people who make the complaint against Mr. Carnegie that he ought to have been satisfied with a smaller fortune and rendered easier the conditions of his work-people. This consummation is not very easily attained, because on a turnover so vast as that of the Carnegie Company the slightest alteration may mean either a large profit or a huge loss. Mr. Carnegie holds his workmen in high appreciation, and he is exceedingly grateful to them for their part in building up his fortune. He acknowledges the severity of their labor, and he always speaks of them in the highest terms of admiration and respect. There is almost a pathetic ring about the following words: "I remember after Vandy and I had gone round the world, and were walking the streets of Pittsburgh, we decided that the Americans were the saddest-looking race we had ever seen. Life is so terribly earnest here. Ambition urges us all on, from him who handles a spade to him who employs thousands. We know no rest."

Mr. Carnegie stands by the fact that he has been instrumental in giving employment to a vast army of workmen. This is his favorite reply to all attacks upon him, and he thinks more of this achievement than he does of all his benefactions. "Those who insure steady employment to thousands at wages not lower than others pay need not be ashamed of their record; for steady employment is, after all, the one indispensable requisite for the welfare and progress of the people."

In addressing his workmen at Pittsburgh in 1893 he said: "I made my first dollar in Pittsburgh, and expect to make my last dollar here also. I do not know any form of philanthropy so beneficial as this: there is no charity in it. I have hoarded nothing, and shall not die rich apart from my interest in the business. Unless the Pittsburgh works are prosperous I shall have nothing. I have put all my eggs in one basket right here, and I have the satisfaction of knowing that the first charge on every dollar of my capital is the payment of the highest earnings paid for labor in any part of the world for similar services. Upon that record I stand."

Andrew Carnegie

CHAPTER VI

CONFLICTS WITH LABOR

LABOR, capital and business ability are the three legs of a three-legged stool. Neither the first, the second nor the third has any preference, all being equally necessary. He who would sow discord among the three is the enemy of all." Thus spoke Andrew Carnegie to an interviewer in March, 1901. Prom time to time he has written freely on the labor question, especially in reference to strikes and trade unions. In 1886 he said: "My experience has been that trade unions upon the whole are beneficial both to labor and capital. They certainly educate the workingman, and give him a truer conception of the relations of capital and labor than he could otherwise form. I recognize in trade unions, or, better still, in organizations of the men of each establishment, who select representatives to speak for them, a means not of further embittering the relations between employer and employed, but of improving them."

Mr. Carnegie thinks that the individual labor organization is the most useful to the workman - that is, each works or groups of works to have their own union which shall be thoroughly cognizant with conditions in its own mill. He does not extend the same approval to the ordinary types of labor organization, nor does he agree with all the principles on which they are founded. When asked whether or not there was in the States an organization known as the "Knights of Labor," which is a similar body to the English trade unions, he replied: "Say rather we had. It was one of those ephemeral organizations that go up like a rocket and come down like a stick. It was founded upon false principles, viz., that they could combine common or unskilled labor with skilled." He holds that the man who is doubly as efficient as another should receive twice as much remuneration, and he continues: "If we are not to recognize that one man has brains or ability beyond another, why should a man of superior parts try to do his best?"

Mr. Carnegie would not tolerate any organization among his work-people that propagated such mischievous principles, and his firm stand on this question was, perhaps, the chief contributing factor to his first dispute with his men. This occurred at his Braddock steel works. It appears that Mr.

Carnegie came to certain terms with his employees which, when embodied in an agreement, the men's leaders refused to sign, incited thereto by the union agitators, at whom the agreement was expressly aimed. The principal feature of the agreement was a substitution of the sliding scale plan of wage-earning for the usual unchanging method. The sliding scale made the workman practically a partner with the company: he either profited or lost with the company. Another feature of the new contract was the abolishment of the eight-hour day - that is, three shifts instead of two to each twenty-four hours. The eight-hour plan was found to be unprofitable and a sliding scale at a twelve-hour schedule was proposed as a substitute. The men were also required to sign a cast-iron agreement promising to abide by the contract for a certain number of years.

These documents were put before the men at the end of the year 1887. During that year it was estimated that Mr. Carnegie had made a profit of $15,000,000. The men refused to agree to the terms set before them, and the works were immediately shut down. No work meant no food, no fuel, no clothes, for everything and everybody in Braddock depended on the mills. All efforts toward compromise on the part of the men were instantly rejected, but no effort was made to replace the locked-out men with outsiders. The men held out from December to April. After unsuccessfully attempting to obtain a settlement on their own lines, the workmen decided to give way, and their leaders waited on Mr. Carnegie with the necessary authority to come to terms, but with the intention of making a nominal surrender only, and not binding themselves personally to the agreement. Mr. Carnegie took the deputation to dinner, joked with them, and then produced the new contracts for their acceptance. The leaders asked if they might be allowed to sign as representatives of the union. "Certainly," said Mr. Carnegie, "you can sign as you please." They signed without hesitation, congratulating themselves on their smartness. "Now," said Mr. Carnegie, "as I have obliged you by letting you sign as you please, would you oblige me by signing in your individual capacity as well?" "Begorrah," said the agitator, "begorrah, the game's up." And it was. They attached their signatures a second time, and the strike was ended.

That is Mr. Carnegie's version of the affair, which, of course, has another aspect when described by the workmen. It was said that the men resumed work on a pledge, given by Mr. Carnegie's manager, that the men thrown out of work by the two-shift instead of the three-shift system would be found employment in the other mills of the company, and that a general amnesty would be granted to all who had taken part in the strike. This pledge, some of the men say, was broken. But there is no evidence that any such pledge was actually given. As a matter of fact, the sliding scale instituted at Braddock has proved uniformly satisfactory to both the workmen and the company, and the plan has been extended to other places.

CARNEGIE INSTITUTE, PITTSBURGH, PA.

The second and last dispute that the Carnegie firm had with its employees was at the Homestead works, over which Mr. Prick, the manager, had supreme control. Owing to the atrocious methods by which the conflict was conducted on both sides, this strike at Homestead caused a sensation throughout the civilized world. As usual there is much contradiction of facts by the parties concerned, and great confusion as to the circumstances of the dispute. The following events are gathered from accounts which were current at the time.

On July I, 1889, the firm made a three-year contract with a number of skilled workmen, through the medium of the Amalgamated Iron and Steel Workers' Association, to pay them at the rate of twenty-five dollars per ton for a certain product of Bessemer steel. At the beginning of June, 1892, Mr. Prick announced that the rate in future would be twenty-two dollars per ton, which he eventually raised to twenty-three dollars, but the men held firm for twenty-four dollars. Mr. Prick further notified them that henceforth the contracts would terminate in midwinter instead of midsummer. The men objected to this because it placed them at a disadvantage.

Negotiations were broken off on June 24th and the mills were shut down on the 30th. Then began a series of heart-rending episodes. Mr. Prick, with an "intelligent anticipation of events" had taken precautionary measures while the negotiations were in progress. He resolved to keep the works going by non-unionist workmen, and to protect these he had engaged three hundred Pinkerton detectives, and had also surrounded the works with fences and trenches until they resembled a military fort. It was reported at the time that along the top of the fence, which was twelve feet high, a barbed wire was laid, which was nicknamed the "live wire fence" because it was charged with a degree of electricity sufficiently strong to kill anyone who touched it. But this was absolutely disproved later. On the other hand, it was stated that the men deliberately attempted to murder all the non-union workmen by poisoning their food as it was being prepared in the kitchens.

Immediately the negotiations in progress between the two parties were ended, the men stationed guards at all the entrances to the mills. The river, the streets and the roads entering the town were also closely patrolled, and a rigid surveillance was exercised over all visitors. During the disturbance great damage was done to the mills of the company and to public property in the town. Prick now thought it was high time to use his police force and attempt the importation of foreign labor. It was arranged that the detectives should proceed to Homestead by the river, and arrive there about midnight, when it was hoped they would be able to enter the works unobserved.

At two o'clock on the morning of July 6, three hundred detectives, accompanied by the deputy-sheriff of the district, embarked on a steamer and two barges and left Pittsburgh for Homestead. On their arrival they found the river banks lined with thousands of men, women, and even children. Many of the men were armed with revolvers and clubs, while the Pinkerton detectives had their Winchester rifles. A short war of words was followed by an attempt of the boating party to land. This was resisted by the frenzied workmen, shots were exchanged, and fighting soon became general. Another determined sortie was made by a body of fifty Pinkertons under cover of the rifle fire from their companions, but they met with such a hot reception that they were compelled to retreat.

The strikers now erected a fort on which they mounted a small piece of artillery and opened fire with it upon the barges. They also endeavored to set fire to the baizes by pouring petroleum in the river, but an unfavorable wind rendered their efforts unsuccessful. The steamer, with the deputy-sheriff and the wounded men on board, got adrift from the two barges, and, running the gantlet of a heavy fire, returned to Pittsburgh. At 5 P. m. on the following day the Pinkertons surrendered on condition that if they gave up their arms they would be guaranteed a safe conduct. Notwithstanding this guarantee, they were brutally assaulted as they passed through the town, and many were seriously injured. The casualties of the whole conflict amounted to six workmen killed and eighteen wounded, nine Pinkertons killed and twenty-one wounded, and a hundred Pinkertons severely mutilated after their surrender.

On learning of the fight, the Governor of the State sent down a force of 8,000 militia, who occupied the works. Rioting, however, continued for a time. On July 23 Mr. Frick was assaulted by a Russian who was admitted to his office on a pretense of business. The loss to the company through the works remaining idle was $50,000 daily, apart from the expense of $20,000 daily for the maintenance of the militia.

A commission was appointed by Congress to institute a thorough inquiry into the whole event, and their report roundly censured everyone concerned, but especially Mr. Frick, at whose door it practically laid the entire responsibility for the conflict. It said: "Mr. Frick seems to have been too stern, brusque, and somewhat autocratic, of which some of the men justly complain. We are persuaded that, if he had chosen, an agreement would have been reached between him and the workmen, and all the trouble which followed would have been avoided."

Professor Bemis, a high authority on industrial problems, and a man universally respected, published an article on the strike which was distinguished by a judicial spirit of impartiality and moderation. He severely condemned the attitude and policy of Mr. Frick, and stated that O'Donnell, the men's representative, made every effort to promote an amicable settlement, and when the negotiations were broken off by Mr. Prick he pleaded for a reopening of the discussion, stating clearly that he believed terms would eventually be agreed upon. But Mr. Frick was obdurate: he had set himself to smash trade unionism.

Attempts were made by the men's leaders to communicate with Mr. Carnegie. Professor Bemis states that O'Donnell applied to Prick for Mr. Carnegie's address in Scotland, which was known only to his business associates. Mr. Frick refused to give the address, whereupon it was obtained from the American Consul in London. The men's terms of settlement were then cabled to Mr. Carnegie, who approved of them and urged an immediate consultation with Frick. Mr. Frick, however, refused to consider the matter at all, and declared that if Carnegie came in person, in company with President Harrison and the entire Cabinet, he would not settle the strike. Mr. Carnegie, in his reply, guarded himself by saying that he had no power to instruct anybody connected with the Carnegie Steel Company. "The officers," he wrote, "are elected for a year, and no one can interfere with them. As for instructing them or compelling them under law to do one thing or another, that is simply an absurd suggestion. I could not if I would, and I would not if I could." This restricted authority is involved in his system of management by partners.

A very different complexion is, however, put upon the outbreak at Homestead by the following summary of events, which is vouched for on the best authority, and which contradicts the personal attacks upon Mr. Carnegie. The issue between the firm and 267 union men, out of 3,000 men employed, was that these malcontents demanded an advance equal to sixty per cent, on the scale, when they were already earning from $10 to $13 per day of eight hours. The firm offered to meet them half way. New machinery, erected at a cost of $4,000,000, had increased the output sixty per cent., and this the firm offered to divide with its union men. When Mr. Carnegie looked, into the matter he pronounced it the most generous offer that had ever been made to employees, as the labor was not harder with the new machinery than with the old.

The firm started the works when the few union men struck, at the wish of the 2,700 others, who offered to work the mills without the union men. It was these latter who, armed with guns and pistols, shot down the police, and so provoked reprisals.

It was the general opinion that if the "little boss," as Mr. Carnegie was called by his men, had been present, the whole matter would have been peacefully settled; but as he was not there it is absurd to charge him with neglect. He did not even hear of it until the works had started. Mr. Frick, as president, with a board of directors, had been in. full control, and the works were running under the protection of the troops of Pennsylvania; the State had the matter in charge.

The chairman of the union publicly stated that in the eyes of the men the trouble never would have happened if Mr. Carnegie had been at home. After it had arisen a committee of workmen wired to Mr. Carnegie: "Kind master, tell us what you want us to do and we will do it"; but the riot had occurred before this telegram had reached him, and had rendered him powerless in the matter.

In the course of his brilliant business career Mr. Carnegie has not had any acute differences with his work-people.

On his return to Pittsburgh in January, 1893, he addressed his employees at Homestead, in the course of his speech saying: "I have not come to Pittsburgh to rake up, but to bury the past. It should be banished as a horrid dream, but the lessons it teaches should be laid to heart for future application. For twenty-six years our concerns have met with only one labor stoppage. I trust and believe that this record will be equaled in the next twenty-five years. When employer and employed become antagonistic their antagonism can only be described as a contest between twin brothers. No genuine victory is possible for either side, only the defeat of both." On all occasions he has emphatically denounced labor disputes, but he does not confine his sympathies entirely to the employers. The following paragraph shows that he is capable of looking at matters sympathetically from the men's standpoint. "When public sentiment has rightly and unmistakably condemned violence, even in the form of which there is the most excuse, I would have the public give due consideration to the terrible temptation to which the workingman on strike is sometimes subjected. To expect that one dependent upon his daily wage for the necessities of life will stand by peaceably and see a new man employed in his stead is to expect much. This poor man may have a wife and children dependent upon his labor. Whether medicine for a sick child, or even nourishing food for a delicate wife is procurable, depends upon his steady employment. In all but a few departments of labor it is unnecessary and, I think, improper to subject men to such an ordeal." He thinks that neither the best men as men nor the best men as workers are thus to be obtained.

Mr. Carnegie has also detailed a number of suggestions for the peaceful settlement of all differences between capital and labor. His main solution of this exceedingly difficult problem is arbitration, work to be continued under old conditions until the arbitrators come to a decision. But he does not state whether arbitration should be compulsory, and thereby he shrinks from grappling with the real difficulty of the situation.

Andrew Carnegie

CHAPTER VII

HIS POLITICAL FAITH

PERHAPS Mr. Carnegie's most striking characteristic is his absolute independence, and in nothing is this more evident than in his political faith. He brings to any subject a vast experience of the world, a shrewd intellect and a forceful will, and irrespective of all other views strikes out his line of thought. Authorities are nothing to him: he totally disregards them; and with a bold originality, that in some instances is almost staggering, he judges a question entirely on its merits as it appeals to his own mind. He pierces the very heart of things, strips a question of all superfluities, and concentrates all his energy on absolute essentials, impatiently brushing to one side all the flummery and fancy work that weave themselves around political issues. Opportunism is abhorrent to him, and he heartily detests the art of "sitting on the fence." The views of such a man are well worthy of critical consideration.

The salient feature of Mr. Carnegie's politics is his passionate devotion to republican government such as is embodied in the Constitution of the United States. In his book, "Triumphant Democracy," and in many magazine articles and interviews, he lauds the glories of American democracy. It is his fetish, and he is an ardent worshiper at its shrine. His views, therefore, on this subject, an English writer says, "are scarcely likely to be well balanced, and, indeed, they resemble more the rhapsodies of an enthusiast than the judgment of a cool, experienced man of the world." The same writer quotes this instance " as an outburst of one-sided sentiment": - "Ah, favored land! The best of the old world seek your shores to swell to still greater proportions your assured greatness. That all come only for the material benefits you confer I do not believe. Crowning these material considerations, I insist that the more intelligent of these people feel the spirit of true manhood stirring within them, and glory in the thought that they are to become part of a powerful people, of a government founded upon the born equality of man, free from military despotism and class distinctions; 117,000 came last month, and the cry is still they come! Oh, ye self -constituted rulers of men in Europe, know you not that the knell of dynasties and of rank is sounding? Are you so deaf that you do not hear the thunders, so blind that you do not see the lightnings which now and then give warning of the storm that is to precede the reign of the people?"

But though in some directions Mr. Carnegie allows himself to go to extremes, in the main his republicanism represents a robust and healthy confidence in an untrammeled democracy. He is a fierce opponent of rank and class distinctions, and he holds in supreme contempt the privileged classes who live a life of selfish luxury, contributing nothing by forced industry or voluntary service to the welfare of society. But he is far from being a socialist, whom he describes as a balloon farmer "wanting to jump to the moon in one bound." His ideal is a government of the people, by the people, for the people.

The House of Lords is to him a monstrosity that ought not to be tolerated for one moment. He holds that its members are drawn from the most incompetent sections of the nation, and that as a whole they are totally unfit to perform legislative functions. He considers that titles have a blighting influence on any one's individuality, and he illustrates his meaning by contrasting the probable places in history of Mr. Gladstone, Lord Beaconsfield and Lord Salisbury. "I have always regarded him (Lord Salisbury) as a striking instance of the advantage of not being born to hereditary wealth and position. Like the great founder of the Cecils, Lord Salisbury himself was born a commoner; a younger son with a younger son's portion, and with the promptings of decided ability in him, he did everything in his power to prevent being narrowed and restricted by the smothering robes of rank and wealth. His country's law forces him to sink his individuality in a peerage, but for which England might have told of a first and second Cecil, as it tells of a first and second Pitt-men too great to be obliterated as men by any title. It is a sad descent in historical rank from 'Cecil' to the Marquis of anything.

"The highest title that a man can write upon the page of history is his own name. Mr. Gladstone's will be there; Gladstone he is; Gladstone he will remain, even if he tried to make future generations lose his commanding personality in the 'Dukedom of Clydesdale or any other title whatever. But who among his contemporaries in public life is to stand this supreme test of masterdom? 'Disraeli' promised well for a time, but he fades rapidly into 'Beaconsfield' - a shadow of a name. The title proves greater than the man."

Mr. Carnegie is an out-and-out radical, and strongly in favor of drastic social reform. But his enthusiasm for Disestablishment, One Man One Vote, Peasant Ownership of Land, etc., is submerged in his passionate antagonism to the principle of monarchical government. "Were I in public life in Great Britain," he writes, "I should be ashamed to waste my energies against the House of Lords, Church and State, primogeniture and entail, and all the other branches of the monstrous system; I should strike boldly at the royal family, the root of the upas tree from which springs all these wrongs."

At one time it was rumored that he intended to enter the British Parliament. That was when Messrs. Bright, Chamberlain, Dilke and Labouchere were fighting hard in the vanguard of extreme radicalism. They had Mr. Carnegie's fullest sympathy and support, and he entertained high hopes that the dawn of republicanism for England was at hand. He was on terms of friendship with all the lights of liberalism in its palmiest days. For Mr. John Morley, and above all for Mr. Gladstone, he had the profoundest respect and admiration, and he regarded Mr. Chamberlain as the coming leader of Democracy and future Prime Minister of England.

He gave expression to this opinion in plain terms in 1885, when he presented copies of Scribner's Statistical Atlas of the United States, showing by graphic methods its political, social, and industrial development.

There is a significance about this incident which it is interesting to recall at the present juncture in English politics, but this does not mean that these views are still held by Mr. Carnegie, who does not now regard the monarchy as a rival to popular self-government.

On a blank page of one atlas he wrote:

"Presented to

THE FREE LIBRARY OP BIRMINGHAM

BY

ANDREW CARNEGIE

Newport, June 9, 1885.

"Let the men of Birmingham note what their kin beyond the sea are doing under Republican institutions founded upon the equality of the Citizen â€" a land where throne and aristocracy are alike unknown.

A. C."

The other atlas he inscribed as follows:

"To
JOSEPH CHAMBERLAIN

The leader of the masses and future Premier
of Britain, I send this record of the reign
of the people under institutions based upon
the only true doctrine, the political equality
of the Citizen.

Andrew Carnegie.

"New York, November 18, 1885."

Four years afterwards Mr. Chamberlain presented this interesting
document as a companion copy to the Birmingham Free Library. A printed
slip announcing the gift was placed inside the atlas for the guidance and
instruction of readers.

HIS POLITICAL FAITH 99

Of English M. P.'s as a whole Mr. Carnegie has no flattering opinion. He
thinks they are sadly lacking in steadfastness, thoroughness and courage.
"So many public men in England 'stoop to conquer,' forgetting that
whatever else they may conquer thereafter they can never conquer that '
stoop ' which drags down their life." And in another place he scoffs at their
timidity. "English politicians are mostly nibblers, small morsels at a time,
though Gladstone can take a good bite when put to it."

Mr. Carnegie applies one principle for the United States and an altogether
different one for Great Britain, because the one had to create manufactures
and the other had them. Take the tariff question. For America he is an out-
and-out Protectionist; for England he is an out-and-out Free Trader. His
arguments in favor of Free Trade for England can be readily agreed with,
but the reasons he originally gave for his support of a protective tariff for
America have long ago disappeared. He maintained that heavy import
duties were necessary in order to enable the American manufacturer to
hold the home market against the foreigner, and he considered his own
industries of iron and steel especially needed this assistance. But to this
view he added the important qualification that he was not in favor of

protection beyond the point necessary to allow America to retain her home market in a fair contest with the foreigner. For the last five years at least the conditions have been exactly the reverse of those put forward by Mr. Carnegie as justifying the McKinley Tariff. Mr. Carnegie, however, though he has not made any appeal for the abolition of the protective duty, has twice advised reductions which were made, and he is in favor of further reductions now. He has been consistent always in this matter, and offended his party, advocating protection only as a path to free trade.

The keynote of one of his most vigorous articles, "What Would I Do with the Tariff if I were Czar?" is the taxing of luxuries, the imported articles the rich consider indispensable and can afford to pay for; on the necessaries of life he would reduce the tariff correspondingly.

Protection or no protection, Andrew Carnegie's genius was bound to lift him to a high position. Much more absurd and much more venomous is the insinuation, at one time freely made in the States, that his influential support of the Republican Party was bought at the price of its adhesion to the McKinley Tariff Bill. That he should be attacked in this way is, perhaps, the natural consequence of his prominence in the political arena. Protection, however, was by no means the subject to which he gave most attention. He attached far more importance to the Silver Question, on which he was one of Mr. Bryan's most formidable antagonists.

Reverting to his interest in British politics, it is interesting to note that, despite his admiration for Mr. Gladstone and his devotion to Mr. Morley, he could not accept unqualified their Irish policy. He was in favor of simply giving Ireland the fullest measure of local self-government, and making her status in the Empire the same as that of a Federal State in the American Union.

A dominating factor in Mr. Carnegie's politics is his love of peace. His hatred and abhorrence of war amounted almost to a passion. In 1881 he said that to him the real glory of America lay in the fact that she had no army worth the name, and that her navy could boast of scarcely a single efficient warship. "What has America to do," he writes, "following in the wake of brutal, pugilistic nations still under the influence of feudal institutions, who exhaust their revenues training men how best to butcher their fellows, and in building ships for purposes of destruction." He has denounced in emphatic terms both the Philippine and South African conflicts as unjust and foolish in the extreme, and he bitterly laments what he considers to be this hateful' relapse of the English-speaking race from its great ideals of peace and freedom. Lifelong Republican though he has been, his feelings on the war policy were so strong that lie severed his allegiance to the Government and ranged himself alongside the Bryanites, to whom he was opposed on every other public question. No one who does not know the exceptional strength of party ties and party loyalty that exist in the United States can understand how keenly such a staunch party man as Andrew Carnegie must have felt this separation from old friends and associations. But holding the views that he did he felt bound to give expression to them. He believed that America was entering upon a policy of imperial expansion and colonial dominion that would lead to a policy of militarism and aggression. Vigorously and vehemently he attacked the Government, and bitterly denounced what he considered its fatal departure from the traditional policy of the nation. He advises both America and Britain to leave the blacks to look after themselves, a sentiment admirably suited for theoretical discussion, but when applied for practical ptirposes it resolves itself into an utter and impossible neglect of duty.

In his political controversies Mr. Carnegie often indulges in prophecies, and one thing he predicted twenty years ago was the decay of Parliament and pulpit and the rise of the newspaper and the review. "The brain of a country," he says, "will be found where the real work is to be done. The House of Lords registers the decrees of the House of Commons. The House of Commons is soon to register the decree of the monthly magazines. In the next generation the debates of Parliament will affect the political currents of the age as little as the fulminations of the pulpit affect religious thought at present. The press is the universal parliament. The leaders in that forum make your statesmen dance as they pipe. If any man wants bona fide substantial power and influence in this world, he must handle the pen - that's flat. Truly it is a nobler weapon than the sword and the tongue, both of which have nearly had their day."

At one time Mr. Carnegie entertained the idea of covering England with a network of Radical newspapers, through which he could impress the masses with his political views. He acquired no less than eighteen organs of the press, but he does not seem to have entered on the work with his usual thoroughness and determination; and although he managed to make a commercial success of the scheme, its political results did not realize expectations.

In regard to religious matters Mr. Carnegie takes up an independent position. He is emphatically not an agnostic. He believes in Christianity and in the goodness of God, but his great human spirit is not to be bound by the formulas of sects and creeds. He tells a very amusing anecdote of an incident that happened when he was traveling in China. He essayed his powers as a missionary on one of the subjects of the Celestial Empire, and the result was not very encouraging for him. He relates the story as follows: "One day I asked our guide, Ah Cum, a gentleman and a scholar, why he did not embrace Christianity. His eyes twinkled as he replied, 'Where goee, eh? Goee Bishopee ? * (pointing to the Cathedral). ' He say allee rightee. Goee there ?' (pointing to the English church). 'Bishopee say damee. Goee Hopper?' (the American Presbyterian missionary). 'He sayee Bishop churchee no goodee, hellee firee. What I doee, eh?' 'Stay where you are, you rogue, ' " replied Mr. Carnegie, and he adds, "Confound that fellow, I did not expect to be picked up in that manner." Mr. Carnegie thinks it is useless to preach to the heathen one God and half a dozen creeds. He considers that to-day the pulpit exercises very little influence on the life of the world. He thinks that its sentiments are practically ignored by men of action and work. "Who cares," he says, "what the Rev. Mr. Froth preaches when he ventures beyond the homilies." He describes the parson to suit him to be one who says little and does much. He has, however, very great faith in the refining and elevating influence of music, which he speaks of as heaven's chief medium.

We have seen that Mr. Carnegie is an optimist of the optimists. The progress of the world and the advance of the English-speaking race are to him as inevitable as that night should follow day, and his faith shines steady and clear through all discouragement. "God's in His heaven, all's right with the world," aptly describes his view of the many mysteries of human life. The following quotation gives one an insight into the standpoint from which he looks out on things: "It is a criminal waste of time and thought to dwell much upon what is to come in the far unknown future. I am an evolutionist. My teacher is Herbert Spencer. It is impossible to set bounds to what the human race can do, or what it may become, physically, mentally, or socially. . . . We are all traveling in the same direction, and finally, I believe, to heaven."

And now we come to the political project which is dearer to Mr. Carnegie than anything else, and to accomplish which he would gladly sacrifice his fortune. Mr. Gladstone once described Mr. Carnegie as so interwoven in his interests between America and England that he formed a living link between them. The one supreme desire of Mr. Carnegie is to weave together the interests of the two nations and form them into one vast confederacy. He is an enthusiastic advocate of the Federation of English-speaking peoples, and he is very sanguine about the possibilities of its achievement, believing that the idea would be heartily welcomed by the vast majority of the people of the United States, and that it would command the enthusiastic support of the colonies. The mother country alone, he thinks, is lukewarm in the matter. It is only in political ideas, he points out, that there is any dissimilarity. In language, literature, religion and law we are a united race. Britain, he maintains, has everything to gain by amalgamation of interests. Her produce would enter the world's finest market - the United States - free of duty, and the accession of strength she would acquire by reunion would relieve her from all fear of European combinations. If England holds back on this vital question, he predicts her downfall from her present proud position as head of the Anglo-Saxon race. "The only course for Britain seems to me to be reunion with her giant child, or sure decline to a secondary place, and then comparative insignificance in the future annals of the English-speaking race."

He looks upon this reunion as the one great hope for the peace and progress of the world. He claims that the welfare of humanity imperatively calls for the consolidation of Anglo-American power. Such a federation would be invincible both in the arts of peace and of war, for it would combine the control of the premier financial and manufacturing resources, with the possession of the finest human material on earth. Its supremacy would be incontestable and would command universal respect. By reason of its power it could set itself up as the arbiter of the world's disputes. The enormous waste of expenditure in maintaining bloated armaments would be stopped, and never again would legalized slaughter of man dishonor the human race.

But is this noble aspiration of Mr. Carnegie's anything more than a castle in the air, and is any progress being made toward its realization? What has he to put forward against the thousand and one practical objections with which his ideal could easily be riddled? First and foremost he sets forth the exigencies of commerce and the blood affinity of the two peoples - the mightiest forces for reunion that could possibly be imagined. In addition to this, Mr. Carnegie regards the abridgment of distance as a favorable factor of much importance. The telegraph and the steamboat have greatly facilitated the means of intercommunication and intervisitation, and travel nowadays is attended with every comfort and luxury. Never was there a time when so many Englishmen and Americans intervisited so often between the two countries. And Mr. Carnegie claims that the stanchest supporters of reunion, and those who are most convinced of its practicability, are to be found among those who have most frequently crossed the "pond" and come into contact with both peoples. The more extensive their knowledge and their travel, the more confirmed are they in their faith. In social life the greatest cordiality exists between the constituents of the two nations, while the masses of both seize every opportunity to express publicly their enthusiasm for the project. "Let men say what they will, therefore," Mr. Carnegie concludes, "I say that as surely as the sun in the heavens once shone upon Britain and America united, so surely it is one morning to rise, shine upon and greet again "The Re-United States," "The British-American Union."

SKIBO CASTLE. MR. CARNEGIE'S HOME IN SCOTLAND

Andrew Carnegie

CHAPTER VIII

INTERNATIONAL COMPETITION

THE race for commercial supremacy between the old and the new world is now the all-engrossing question of the hour. The last generation has witnessed a remarkable change in the rapid advance which the traders of the West have made upon the markets of the world. The development of the United States as a trade competitor with European countries is the most conspicuous landmark in the commercial history of the nineteenth century. Supported by unlimited natural resources, it has made enormous strides as a manufacturing country. Its citizens, buoyant with youthful energy and ambition, have utilized to the full every advantage within their power. Armed with the latest weapons they have successfully attacked foreign markets, and to-day American manufacturers hold a strong position in almost every commercial corner in the world. This wonderful progress has been due to several causes, prominent among which are its enormous mineral wealth, cheap locomotion, protectionist duties, a dogged enterprise, and an inherent commercial skill.

No American has made such an impress upon the trade of the world as Andrew Carnegie. The greatest iron and steel producer, he has led the American attack on all the markets in its most important sphere, namely, the region of iron and steel manufacture. The prosperity of a manufacturing country is to be measured in the main by the prosperity of its iron and steel industries, and it is in this realm of industry that Andrew Carnegie has earned his title of King. His ability to deliver promptly owing to his skillfully equipped works, and the low price he could accept as a result of having at his elbow cheap material and quick facilities for production, gave him an immense advantage over his competitors. He conducted his business on a large scale, fully confident of securing a fair share of the world's patronage. His strong faith told him to cast his net, and he obeyed. The harvest he has brought safely to land is now the admiration of the whole world. Having won a great industrial victory, Mr. Carnegie should be in an authoritative position to speak upon the present state of trade and the commercial prospects of the old and new worlds. His innate sense of justice, his well-balanced intellect and his wide experience entitle his views to careful consideration. Although a Scotchman by birth, hard-headed, thrifty and industrious, Mr. Carnegie is by training a typical American. He has won his fortune in the land of big things, and it is only natural he should have a very high opinion of America's industrial resources and commercial future. He considers the United States in many respects far ahead of Great Britain, and holds that really the mother country will have to bestir itself if it is even to occupy a second place on the list. "The Briton has now," he says, "to meet in industrial rivalry men of his own blood; what is more, men of his own blood developed under more favorable circumstances." But although he considers the American workman "the ablest, quickest and most versatile worker the world has ever seen," he at the same time believes the old country will yet make a gallant struggle, especially if she will change her methods and show more enterprise. America has the great advantage that "whereas her resources have only been scratched, as it were, the raw materials of the old country are rapidly being worked out."

Probably very few Britons will agree with his gloomy view of the future, when he pictures their islands as the ancestral home and the garden and pleasure-ground of the race. This elysium is to come into existence when "British manufactures have gone one by one," and when, as a nation, "we shall not be able to support a population of more than fifteen millions."

He contributed a practical and stable article to the pages of the *Nineteen Century and After* review for June, 1901, and one which, although somewhat unpalatable to the imperialistic taste, contained much food for thought. The article was couched in a more optimistic strain, and made a bold attack on "British Pessimism," which he was surprised to find had obtained such a strong hold on English industrial life. Although he has visited his native land for thirty years or more, he could not recollect having met with such a state of despondency amongst the leaders of British industries. But continuing, he immediately strikes a cheerful note, and says that "though your monopoly has gone your supremacy has not; that so far there is no actual retrogression or inherent decay."

Mr. Carnegie is of the opinion that England's legislators would spend their time more profitably if they paid more attention to commercial affairs and less to political wrangling. He argues that "a profitable home market is the strongest weapon that can be used to conquer markets abroad." The qualities of the race, he says, "lie dormant, and are still there; the dogged endurance, the ambition to excel, the will to do or die, are all there, but it has not been found necessary to drill them into disciplined action."

Not until British manufacturers are face to face with ruin, and are compelled for lack of work to close their mills, does Mr. Carnegie think they will rouse themselves from their lethargy born of custom and monopoly. When this hour arrives he little doubts that they will rise to the occasion and manifest to the world their true qualities; but by that time he is very much afraid the financial burdens of the country will be so heavy that they will be unable to make up their lost ground. He regards with misgiving "the aggressive temper which has alienated other governments and peoples, and mistaken territorial acquisition for genuine empire building." This dangerous growth, he maintains, will not only largely increase the nation's financial burdens, but will deprive it of its productive capacity and decrease its volume of trade. If ever a nation had a clear and unmistakable warning that the time had arrived when it should henceforth measure its responsibilities and ambitions throughout the world with its resources, and cut its garment according to its cloth, Mr. Carnegie thinks, it is "the dear old mother-land of the race, with its trade stationary and an army of thirty thousand men or more to be provided for in South Africa even after peace comes; its expenditures and taxation increasing, and its promises to pay already at such a discount as to attract capital from across the Atlantic."

He has often pointed out that in the United States and Germany the controlling factor of diplomacy is the expansion of trade. Mr. Carnegie looks at this question in the dry light of hard business experience, and the test he applies to the policy of Great Britain is - "Does it pay?" This test may seem harshly materialistic, but this is a materialistic world, and however glorious may be her traditions, however extensive may be her empire, however powerful may be her army and navy, if Great Britain loses her trade these things cannot prevent her downfall. To-day commerce is the life-blood of a nation, and should be regarded as its paramount consideration. This fact has been lost sight of in the territorial expansion of Great Britain. They go to an enormous expense in opening up vast territories and in conquering subject races, but they receive no corresponding compensation under their policy of free trade which gives the German and American equal commercial opportunities with themselves. They acquire shadowy supremacy with- out any material benefits. *"Trade does not follow the flag,"* Mr. Carnegie argues; *"it follows the lowest price current."*

The gist of his argument is that Great Britain should have a Minister of Commerce, whose special work would be to protect the interests of British traders, and utilize to the full for commercial purposes their world-wide possessions. This office will no doubt be created when international competition has captured more of their markets abroad.

Foreign trade has not such a strong fascination for Mr. Carnegie as may be supposed. He told the Institute of Civil Engineers, in May, 1901, "You must look at home, and develop the material you have there. The way to get hold of foreign markets is to get hold of and conquer the markets at home."

Commercial supremacy and commercial education are indissolubly linked together, and when we turn to examine Mr. Carnegie's views on education we find much that is worthy of notice. We have already mentioned his firm belief that the policy he pursued of throwing responsibility upon young men and taking those of exceptional ability into partnership has contributed more than anything else to his success in business. It is not the unrivaled resources of America the English have cause to envy most, he says, nor its wonderful machinery, but the class of young men that manage the undertakings there, and, he adds, he can find no such class in England. The reason why English young men are not the equals, in his opinion, to their American cousins is simply because they have not had the same educational opportunities.

"It is a result of your System of education," he told a representative of the *Daily News Weekly*. "The universities of America do not exalt science above classics, but they do place them upon a more equal footing than you do. Classical subjects have received encouragement and have been developed, whereas scientific education has not been. Now, I believe that the continuance of Great Britain as one of the principal manufacturing nations will not be secured by having a greater number of her people learning the dead languages of dead nations, dwelling together in the past, but by a larger percentage of her young men becoming experts in various branches of science, and being taught to be scientific managers of her industries, displacing the rule of thumb managers. It is a question what type of a man is now needed to keep England abreast of her competitors."

In connection with this question of trade supremacy, the following information relating to commercial education in America will be of interest. No less than five of the leading colleges and universities of the United States have given a place in their curriculum to commercial courses or have established Schools of Commerce. The students are given a course of teaching comprising the most serviceable instruction in the following subjects: bookkeeping, commercial geography, transport systems, money and banking, business organization and management, economics and economic history. In addition, it is recognized that the prospective manufacturer should be familiar with the various processes through which the chief articles of commerce have to pass before they reach their finished state. This knowledge is imparted through a course on "The Materials of Commerce," which is illustrated as far as possible by practical experiments. A knowledge of law is a further advantage to a business man, and this is provided by courses on commercial law, tariff legislation, and the laws pertaining to labor, capital and corporations. The usual instruction in modem languages, chemical research and physical science is given, and students are at liberty to study for a particular trade or for work in a foreign country. Candidates for a degree must pass in all these branches.

A thorough commercial education is the strongest foundation for business success, but Mr. Carnegie believes that another phase of knowledge is also requisite. He says: "The study of human nature is the best education for any business man. But whether a young man chooses a scientific or a classical education, if he wishes to pursue a business career he should not remain long at college or at the university. All my brilliant partners began hard, practical work in their teens. I think a course at a modem university from nineteen to twenty-four will not teach a young fellow to be as successful a business man as if he had been sent into business in a subordinate capacity. This is not disparaging university education, for I limit the observation to the business career."

Mr. Carnegie is, above everything else, a man of action. He is a self-made millionaire, and has built up his huge fortune by the power of his brain; it is therefore only natural he should have a strong admiration for those who seek practical experience and are desirous of adding to their knowledge by contact with hard work. He has, however, a strong faith in education, as was so strikingly illustrated by his munificent gifts of $250,000 to the Birmingham University, $10,000,000 for the Scotch universities and $10,000,000 to the Carnegie Institute, and in this sphere it may be taken for granted he will distribute a large share of his wealth. Compared with other nations Mr. Carnegie recognizes the backward state of technical education in England, and if they are to retain their commercial position he thinks it will be absolutely necessary for them to overhaul and modernize their educational machinery and to put it in proper and efficient working order. To keep in the forefront of the international trade fight will mean a stem struggle, but it can be accomplished, he sa3rs, if Britain goes to the root of the question and arms the rising generation with a sound and practical education. In the letter he sent to the Right Hon. Joseph Chamberlain, M. P., offering to give $250,000 to the funds of the Birmingham University, he stated his views on commercial education in a very plain and businesslike manner.

"Dear Mr. Chamberlain: - You have interested me in your proposed university at Birmingham for the people of the Midlands.

"May I suggest that an opportunity exists for such an institution to perform a great service for the whole country?

"After the members of the Iron and Steel Institute had returned to New York from their tour of observation through the United States, the officials dined with me. Many pleasing short speeches were made. The close of one I have never forgotten. A partner in one of your foremost steel companies said: 'Mr. Carnegie, it is not your wonderful machinery, not even your unequaled supplies of minerals, which we have most cause to envy. It is something worth both of these combined - the class of scientific young experts you have to manage every department of your works. We have no corresponding class in England.'

"Never were truer words spoken. Now this class you must sooner or later secure if Britain is to remain one of the principal manufacturing nations, and it seems to me the Midlands is the very soil upon which it can most surely be produced.

"If I were in your place I should recognize the futility of trying to rival Oxford and Cambridge, which, even if possible, would be useless. The twin seats of learning have their mission, and fulfil it; but Birmingham should make the scientific the principal department, the classical subsidiary. If Birmingham were to adopt the policy suggested, taking our Cornell University as its model, where the scientific has won first place in the number of students, and give degrees in science as in classics, I should be delighted to contribute the last £50,000 of the sum you have set out to raise, to establish a scientific department.

"I am sure our people of the Birmingham across the Atlantic will heartily approve this gift to their prototype on this side of the water, for what does not the younger owe of its greatness and prosperity to the old land. Bessemer, Siemens, Thomas - the triumvirate through whose inventions we have been enabled to make and sell steel by the millions of tons at three pounds for a penny - all made their experiments in your midst.

"Let the gift, therefore, be considered as only a slight acknowledgment of a debt which Pittsburgh, the greatest beneficiary of your steel inventions, can never hope to repay.

"Wishing you speedy success,

"Sincerely yours,

"Andrew Carnegie."

The object of this broad-minded millionaire is to place before the youth of Britain the same educational opportunities as are enjoyed by young men in the United States and on the Continent. If words of warning and magnificent pecuniary assistance can rouse his native land to make adequate preparations for commercial training, he should be eminently successful. He lays great stress on the need of giving the young men who are to be the future captains of industry a suitable and practical education. Much depends on the artisan, he once said, but still more depends on the commercial skill of the man at the wheel. Clever managers with up-to-date methods and modem ideas will be almost certain to secure good paying orders, and it is this class of men he desires to see controlling England's industries; and then he has little doubt she will hold her own against the competition of the world. In Mr. Carnegie's opinion England's national industries are at the present time handicapped greatly by obsolete machinery. Their equipments, he says, need not merely to be altered but "revolutionized." In one of his journeys through England he came across a tanyard in charge of which was a workman of the extreme rural type, who informed Mr. Carnegie that his old master had just sold out. The fresh owner had new-fangled notions, and was spending "heaps o' money" in building a steam-engine, which he invited the visitor to inspect. This engine was expected to do the work much quicker, but, remarked the old work- man, "I've heard tell by some as knows it's na sae gud for the leather." This incident, Mr. Carnegie says, aptly illustrates the tenacity with which Britishers hold to what their fathers did before them. Although somewhat exaggerated, this conclusion contains much truth, and the ill-advised obstinacy of the British workman and the short-sighted policy of trade unionism is largely answerable for it. Mr. Carnegie absolutely fought trade unionism in his own works, when it attempted to encumber him with restrictions and to dictate to him how he should manage his business.

For the saner type of trade unionism, as we have seen, he has considerable sympathy. The American workman comes up to his ideal as the quickest and most versatile industrial hand in the world. In sharp contrast to his prototype in England, he is distinguished for his habits of sobriety and thrift, and these, in Mr. Carnegie's opinion, largely account for his superiority. England's drink bill per head of the population is nearly fifty per cent, higher than that of the United States, and to this marked difference he attributes their inferiority to the Yankee in business foresight and industrial skill.

But the faults of the working classes by no means exonerate the masters from blame. It is, indeed, in fertility and originality of ideas that Brother Jonathan so easily surpasses England. They are fearfully slow, Mr. Carnegie says, in adopting new improvements, and pointing to electricity as a concrete instance, and referring to the achievements of Edison, "the wizard of science," he mentions the significant fact that a capital of over $200,000,000 is invested in about 20,000 miles of electric railways in the United States. England is just awakening to the value of this form of locomotion, and so far nearly all the great electrical undertakings in England are worked by American capital. But where British manufacturers are most heavily handicapped is in their means of transport. The "miserable little trucks on your railways and the extortionate charges" fill Mr. Carnegie with disgust and amazement. He once said that if all the existing rolling stock in England were destroyed it would be a blessing to British industry rather than a calamity.

His views on this great question of International Competition as it affects British interests have been severely criticized, but there is no denying the fact that many of his suggestions and opinions contain much sound common sense and are of much practical value. He is a man of conviction, and having satisfied himself upon the justness of his cause, is not afraid to express his views. He is a candid friend to his native land, and all who are open to conviction will thank him for the genuine interest and thoughtful counsel. Britain could do with more men of Mr. Carnegie's caliber, who put duty and conviction before fame and applause. British manufacturers can draw many valuable lessons from his industrial methods and his views on the question of International Competition.

CHAPTER IX

HIS GOSPEL OF WEALTH

IT is rare indeed to hear "the advantages of poverty" eulogized by a millionaire. In a world where selfish interests are everywhere pursued it seems almost an irony to ask anyone to believe that a man with unfettered millions can delight to sing its praises and to condemn those who hoard wealth from selfish motives. Of all the puzzling paradoxes surely this is the greatest! At first sight it would seem that the author of such a doctrine must be a confirmed miser. But Mr. Carnegie is neither a millionaire miser nor a meddling moralizer, for if any man practises what he preaches, that man is Andrew Carnegie. Yet he is not a philanthropist. He lays no claim to such a title. A philanthropist he defines as a man who gives his wealth and follows it up by personal labor. Mr. Carnegie has given vast sums away, but he has not carried out the second stipulation, and therefore the honor of being styled "a philanthropist" is not, he says, his right. As it would be impossible for him to concentrate his energies upon one particular kind of work, owing to the enormous amount of labor involved in the distribution of his fortune, he has an excellent excuse, and we must forgive him for his modest interpretation of the title. But if he is not a philanthropist, what is he? *A trustee for the English-speaking race.* Wealth he says, should be held in trust for the benefit of the whole community. Attached to its ownership are great responsibilities, and if the millionaire fails to carry them out it will be counted by future generations as a gross neglect of public duty.

Mr. Carnegie's gospel has many different aspects, but it falls into two main parts: the advantages of poverty and the responsibilities of surplus wealth. His views on the distribution of wealth have always excited a good deal of interest. They are distinguished by characteristic thoroughness, striking originality, lofty ideals and a large-hearted spirit; and coming from one who is a millionaire many times over, it is only natural they should have attracted world-wide attention V Mr. Carnegie during the last fifteen years has written several prominent articles on the subject of wealth, and given expression to his views in a number of speeches and conversations. He was asked some years ago, "What are the gifts a youth, who has the ambition to make millions, should be endowed with at his birth?" The steel millionaire replied: "The greatest of all advantages with which he can begin life is that of being poor. The man who wishes to make millions should not be born with a silver spoon in his mouth. He must feel that it is sink or swim with him. He must start his life with no bladders, no life-preservers, no support. "This advice is characteristic of its giver, and there is no doubt as to the conviction which inspired it.

The same may be said of all Mr. Carnegie's views. He holds that there is no better schoolmaster than adversity, and that the youth who has witnessed the struggles of his parents against poverty's hardships has had the best of all incentives to success. Having driven the wolf from the door of his own home, he can speak from actual experience, and though many will find themselves unable to follow Mr. Carnegie all the way, yet it cannot be denied that if poverty teaches nothing else it impresses the virtue of thrift, and in some cases, but not all, urges a youth to make his position in the world by industrious and honorable effort. When Mr. Carnegie refers to the "poor" boy he does not mean the unfortunate urchins of slumland, who are reared amid the vilest surroundings of immorality and filth. To contend that such conditions were "advantageous" would be absurd. To quote his own words: "It is not so much to raise the submerged tenth, but to help the swimming tenth to keep their heads above water." It is the members of this "swimming tenth" - in other words, the industrious poor, who have to struggle hard day by day to earn an honest living, and who try, little by little, to improve their position, that Mr. Carnegie is concerned with.

In 1891 he contributed an article on "The Advantages of Poverty" to the *Nineteenth Century Review*, in which he dealt at considerable length with the question of hereditary wealth and the influence of home life on the careers of young men. Poor boys reared by their parents have, he maintained, many advantages over those taught by hired strangers and exposed to the temptations of wealth; and to him it is not surprising that they become "the leaders in every branch of human action." He pictures them as athletes trained for the contest, with "sinews braced, indomitable wills, resolved to do or die." Such boys, he says, "always have marched and always will march straight to the front and lead the world; they are the epoch-makers." The men who have lifted and advanced the race and been supremely great in every field of human triumph, he argues, have not been those endowed with wealth and hereditary rank, the possession of which "is almost fatal to greatness and goodness," but young men who have been nurtured "in the bracing school of poverty - the only school capable of producing the supremely great, the genius."

Mr. Carnegie's glowing defense of poverty's blessings is open to argument; but nevertheless we cannot but admire his ardent enthusiasm and strong convictions. Poverty has an altogether opposite effect on different natures, and in some cases its environment acts as a wet blanket on youthful hopes, and its menial work tends to blunt the intellect and overtax the physical and moral strength. Mr. Carnegie's career is a singular exception. We cannot judge by one particular instance, but apply the principles generally. With a feeling of sincere pleasure we quote the following paragraph from an article by one who has experienced all the bitterness of a hard struggle with poverty and, while successful in his fight for fortune, has retained intact the simplicity of his soul amid all the enticements of superfluous wealth. "Among many advantages arising, not from the transmission of hereditary wealth and position, but from the transmission of hereditary poverty and health, there is one which, to my mind, outweighs all the others combined. It is not permitted the children of king, millionaire or noble to have father and mother in the close and realizing sense of these sacred terms. The name of father and the holier name of mother are but names to the child of the rich and the noble. To the poor boy these are the words he conjures with, his guides, the anchors of his soul, the objects of his adoration. Neither nurse, servant, governess nor tutor has come between him and his parents. In his father he has had tutor, companion, counselor and judge. It is not given to the born millionaire, noble or prince to dwell upon such an inheritance as is his who has had in his mother, nurse, seamstress, teacher, inspirer, saint - his all in all."

Mr. Carnegie's whole article was distinguished by great force and clearness. It consisted chiefly of a spirited reply to Mr. Gladstone's and the Rev. Hugh Price Hughes's criticisms upon his famous article "Wealth," which appeared in the North American Review for June, 1889. This created a great sensation at the time of its publication, and drew forth comments from a number of public men in England and America, prominent among whom were President Cleveland, Cardinal Manning, Rabbi Adler, Cardinal Gibbons and Bishop Potter. It formed the topic of a comprehensive discussion in the principal reviews and newspapers, and though generally commended, it did not escape trenchant criticism from some quarters.

We would have liked to have quoted in full many striking passages from this article, but must be content with some brief extracts. At the present time, when Mr. Carnegie is just entering upon the gigantic task of distributing his wealth and carrying into practice the principles he then laid down, his written views on the subject possess additional importance. The three articles he has written on the influence and use of wealth will repay study by those who are interested in the great social questions of the hour.

SKIBO CASTLE. VIEW FROM THE WOOD

The article opened with a reference to the changed conditions of industrial life and the transference of labor from the home to the factory. He ridiculed the suggestion of "good old times," and strongly maintained that every section of society is now living under happier and better conditions. The laborer has now more comforts than the farmer had a few generations ago, and the farmer more than the landlord previously enjoyed. These changed conditions have caused a division between employer and employee, but this, he holds, has not been without its good results. The law of competition is now the dominating influence in the commercial world, and "the survival of the fittest" the recognized basis of individual action. He quoted the maxim, "If thou dost not sow, thou shalt not reap," and gave a well-deserved reproof to the growth of idleness and wasteful luxury. Socialistic theories which mean "revolution, not evolution," were severely treated. "There can never be equality of power or pay in this world," he wrote, "where individualism is necessary to its progress and proper government."

He then went on to state that there are three modes in which surplus wealth can be distributed. It can be left to the family, or bequeathed for public purposes, or administered during their lives by its possessors. Under the first and second modes most of the world's wealth has been applied. Both, in Mr. Carnegie's opinion, are injudicious, and especially the custom of leaving wealth to the eldest son, which, he says, is done simply to gratify the family pride of maintaining titles intact. To leave fortunes to children is "to impose upon them a burden and a disadvantage." This assertion bears the stamp of originality, but we are afraid it will not find many disciples among modem millionaires. "Beyond providing for the wife and daughters moderate sources of income, and a very moderate allowance indeed, if any, for the sons, men may well hesitate, for it is no longer questionable that great sums bequeathed oftener work more for injury than for benefit to the recipient. Wise men will soon decide that for the best interests of the members of their own families and of the State such bequests are an improper use of their means." Mr. Carnegie believes in the millionaire giving his son a good and efficient education, and, if he enters public life, according him proper support ; but to the idle spendthrift he would not give a penny, idleness and waste he detests, and he is never tired of denouncing these abuses in rich and poor alike. Work is the oxygen of a happy and contented life, and without it man degenerates. The indolent and listless habits of the modem "aristocratic" young man form a typical illustration.

Mr. Carnegie is strongly in favor of death duties. First, because they are a profitable source of income for the State; and, secondly, because men should dispose of their surplus wealth while living. He thus characterizes the leaving of wealth for special uses: "As to the second mode, that of leaving wealth at death for public uses, it may be said that this is only a means for the disposal of wealth, provided a man is content to wait until he is dead before he becomes much good in the world."

He can see no grace in the gifts of a man who, unable to take his money with him, is compelled, by mere force of circumstances, to make some bequests before he dies. The man who leaves his wealth at death "erects a monument to his own folly," for it is very seldom his expressed desires are realized afterward. "By taxing estates heavily at death, the State marks its condensation of the selfish millionaire's unworthy life."

Mr. Carnegie holds that the man of wealth should personally superintend the distribution of his assets. To quote again from the article :

"There remains, then, only one mode of using great fortunes; but in this we have the true antidote for the temporary unequal distribution of wealth, the reconciliation of the rich and the poor - a reign of harmony another ideal, differing, indeed, from that of the Communist in requiring only the further evolution of existing conditions, not the total overthrow of our civilization. It is founded upon the present most intense individualism, and the race is prepared to put it in practice by degrees whenever it pleases. Under its sway we shall have an ideal State, in which the surplus wealth of the few will become, in the best sense the property of the many, because administered for the common good; and this wealth, passing through the hands of the few, can be made a much more potent force for the elevation of our race than if distributed in small sums to the people themselves. Even the poorest can be made to see this, and to agree that great sums gathered by some of their fellow citizens and spent for public purposes, from which the masses reap the principal benefit, are more valuable to them than if scattered among themselves in trifling amounts through the course of many years.

He says: "It is well to remember that it requires the exercise of not less ability than that which acquired the wealth to use it so as to be *really beneficial* to the community." That is one of the most significant tenets of his gospel, and those wiseacres who take such supreme delight in offering the Laird of Skibo advice, and proposing to him schemes, would save themselves much time and disappointment if they made a note of this decisive principle, and the fact that Mr. Carnegie has an unbroken law "to help only those who help themselves."

Rich men, he says, have cause to be thankful for one inestimable boon - "they have it in their power, during their lives, to busy themselves in organizing benefactions from which the masses of their fellows will derive lasting benefit, and thus they will dignify their own lives."

One of the most striking passages in the article was the one which denounced indiscriminate charity. "It were better for mankind that the millions of the rich were thrown into the sea than so spent as to encourage the slothful, the drunken, the unworthy. Of every thousand dollars spent in so-called charity to-day, it is probable that nine hundred and fifty dollars are unwisely spent - so spent, indeed, as to produce the very evils which it hopes to mitigate or cure." Business methods are indispensable, he maintains, in the task of distributing wealth. Before a gift is made the donor should institute inquiries to find out if the object is worthy of support. This is a rule which, though liable to err on the side of severity, has many sound recommendations, and is likely to be mo^ generally adopted in the future by men of wealth, Mr. Carnegie has an idea that many well-meant bequests greatly encourage idleness, and rather support those who " neither toil nor spin," he would keep his millions under lock and key.

While approving of Mr. Carnegie's businesslike methods in the distribution of his wealth, many think he would be well advised to widen his horizon and take a more liberal view of the world's voluntary work. So far his attention has been confined to one particular comer. That is a very promising field, and one of the most worthy, there is no doubt, but yet there are other plots which have very strong claims, and only need developing to yield abundant harvests. With more leisure to look around, he will doubtless discover some of the good qualities which distinguish other noble branches of social work in which self-help is the sustaining force.

Mr. Carnegie has laid down what he considers to be the *duty* of the man of wealth. "First, to set an example of modest, unostentatious living, shunning display and extravagances; to provide moderately for the legitimate wants of those dependent upon him ; after doing so to consider all surplus revenues which come to him simply as trust funds, which he is called upon to administer, and strictly bound as a matter of duty to administer, in the manner which in his judgment is best calculated to benefit the community. The man of wealth thus becomes the mere agent and *trustee* for his poorer brethren, bringing to their service his superior wisdom, experience and ability to administer, and doing for them better than they would or could do for themselves.

;

This is a high-minded ideal scheme of excellent merits, and when the world's millionaires embrace it one and all we shall look with greater faith to that

"One far off divine event
To which the whole nation moves."

That his gospel is sound and practicable the world has already had many convincing proofs, not the least in scope and results being Mr. Carnegie's own benefactions. He has written a list of commandments, specially suited for millionaires, and we trust his gospel will yet find many adherents. One thing is certain, those who follow it will write their names indelibly upon their country's history, and be venerated by succeeding generations.

Mr. Carnegie has given his gospel the best possible christening, and there are significant signs that he is likely to have many worthy followers. While millions are a burden to some men, and crush both soul and energy, he finds in them no source of anxiety. They are his, and yet they are not. Their disbursement will give him the greatest happiness and abolish all thoughts of anxiety from his mind.

Mr. Carnegie has taken a glimpse into the future, when he hopes the problem of rich and poor will be solved. "The laws of accumulation and distribution, "he says, " will be left free. Individualism will continue, but the millionaire will be but a trustee for the poor, entrusted for a season with a great part of the increased wealth of the community and administering it for that community far better than it could or would have done for itself. A stage in the development of the race will thus be reached, when it will be clearly seen that there is no mode of disbursing surplus wealth creditable to thoughtful, earnest men into whose hands it flows, save by using it year by year for the general good."

Mr. Carnegie thinks this new era in the world's history has already dawned; and as the light becomes more distinct he prophecies that the voice of the people will strongly condemn the man who hoards wealth instead of wisely allotting it to better his fellow men. Making handsome bequests before the last hour will not earn the full reward. Giving during life is, in his opinion, the only just and proper course.

"The day is not far distant," he says, "when the man who dies, leaving behind him millions of available wealth, which was free for him to administer during life, will pass away unwept, unhonored and unsung, no matter to what use he leaves the dross which he can-not take with him. Of such as these the public verdict will be: '*The man who dies thus rich dies disgraced.*' Such, in my opinion, is the true gospel concerning wealth, obedience to which is destined some day to solve the problem of rich and poor, and to bring peace on earth and goodwill to men."

This noble ideal, drawn so vividly and urged so forcibly by the Pittsburgh millionaire, is what the world is waiting to see realized. Mr. Carnegie has already proved by practice that he believes in his great ideal. It is something more than words to him. He is convinced that it can be applied, and now that he has cut himself clear from all business duties, and has at his unrestricted command more than $250,000,000, the world may expect some epoch-making announcements during the next few years.

In his review of the "Gospel of Wealth," Mr. Gladstone hailed Mr. Carnegie as a philanthropist of the highest order: "This self-made millionaire has confronted the moral and social problem of wealth more boldly, so far as I know, than any previous writer. His courage and frankness, both of them superlative, are among the attendant virtues which walk in the train of munificence not less modest and simple than it is habitual and splendid."

The Rev. Hugh Price Hughes, in commenting upon Mr. Carnegie's "Gospel of Wealth," asserted that "the progress of millionaires is inevitably accompanied by the growing poverty of their fellow-countrymen."

To this line of argument Mr. Carnegie made a very powerful reply. "The progress and the evolution of the millionaire," he insisted, " is beneficial to the whole community. So far from it being a fact that 'millionaires at one end of the scale mean paupers at the other/ the reverse is obviously true. In a country where millionaires exist there is very little excuse for pauperism. Millionaires can only grow amid general prosperity, and this is largely promoted by their exertions. Their profits accrue in periods when wages are high, and the higher the wages that have to be paid the higher the revenues of the employer." The Rev. Mr. Hughes, in his criticism, also said that in a State under really Christian principles "a millionaire would be an impossibility." Mr. Carnegie neatly retorted that there would also be "no need for parsons," and he jocularly added, "the successors of Mr. Hughes and myself, arm-in-arm, will make a pretty pair, out in search of some light work with heavy pay."

In the *North American Review* for 1891, Mr. Carnegie wrote a second article on his "Gospel of Wealth." It was characterized by the same earnest spirit and businesslike suggestions, and consisted in the main of a scheme by which the millionaire could, to the advantage of the community, distribute his wealth. He again severely chastised the miser for his sins. Mr. Carnegie is thoroughly well versed in Biblical quotations, and very often when speaking or writing he repeats some well-known passage of Scripture, and draws his similes from the best of all books, but not always with due reverence. "There will be nothing to surprise the student of socialistic development," he wrote, "if society could approve the text which says that a camel can go through the eye of a needle more easily than a rich man can enter the kingdom of heaven."

In the course of the article Mr. Carnegie dealt with seven objects which, in his opinion, were worthy of the attention of those possessed of wealth, (I) To found or enlarge a university ; (2) The erection of free libraries; (3) Establishment of hospitals or laboratories; (4) To present public parks; (5) to open public halls with organs; (6) To start swimming baths; (7) To build churches.

At a time when all the world is wondering how he will dispose of his surplus wealth, his views as to the merits of these channels of usefulness will be interesting:

To found or enlarge a University.

"Standing apart by itself there is the founding of a university by men enormously rich. By adding to and extending those universities in existence a wide field remains for the millionaire as distinguished from the Croesus among millionaires."

To found Free Libraries.

"The result of my own study of the question: What is the best gift that can be given to a community? is, that a free library occupies the first place, provided that the community will accept and maintain it as a public institution, as much a part of the city property as its public schools, and indeed an adjunct to those. Closely allied to the library, and, where possible, attached to it, there should be rooms for an art gallery and museum, and a hall for such lectures and instruction as are provided in the Cooper Union."

To establish Hospitals and Laboratories.

"We have another most important department in extension of hospitals, medical colleges, laboratories, and other institutions connected with the alleviation of human suffering, and especially with the prevention rather than the cure of human ills. The forms that benefactions to these may take are numerous, but probably none is more useful than that of building schools for the training of female nurses."

To present Public Parks.

"In the very front rank of benefactions public parks should be placed, always provided that the community undertakes to maintain, beautify and preserve inviolate the parks given to it."

To open Public Halls with Organs.

"We have another good use for surplus wealth in providing for our cities halls suitable for meetings of all kinds, especially for concerts of elevating music. Our cities are rarely provided with halls for these purposes. The gift of a hall to any city lacking one is an excellent use of surplus wealth for the good of a community, provided the city agrees to maintain and use it."

To erect Swimming Baths.

"In another respect we are still much behind Europe, A form of beneficence which is not uncommon there is providing swimming baths for the people."

To build Churches.

"Churches as fields for surplus wealth have purposely been reserved until the last, because, these being sectarian, every man will be governed by his own attachments; therefore it may be said gifts to churches are not in one sense gifts to the community at large, but to special classes. The millionaire should not figure how cheaply this structure can be built, but how perfect it can be made. But, having given the building, the donor should stop there; the support of the church should be upon its own people. There is not much genuine religion in the congregation or much good to flow from the church which is not supported at home."

With this last statement there will be a general agreement. A religion bereft of self-sacrificing charity is not worthy of the name. Mr. Carnegie has given liberally to many of the objects specified in this article, including the presentation of some hundreds of organs to places of worship and public halls; but he has yet to build his first church. The main reasons for his abstinence from this branch of philanthropy are the narrowness and sectarianism which distinguishes the church of the present day. A united church, with one plain form of religion, would probably find in Mr. Carnegie a generous supporter ; but while there are so many sects, so many divisions, so many conflicting creeds, it is impossible for one of a very broad mind and national sympathies to give his money to one particular branch of religion. So he holds himself aloof, leaving the work to those who have more faith in their self -chosen mode of worship.

It is a matter of general surprise that Mr. Carnegie has not helped any branch of church work, and there have been many hasty judgments passed upon his attitude by good people, who have written him long letters asking for support toward "their forthcoming bazaar or church extension scheme," but to their disappointment and vexation no notice has been taken of their carefully posted epistles. A little thought and study of the man and his views would have convinced the good-hearted letter-writer that to build hopes of receiving either help or a reply would be entirely delusive. Nothing can be lost by asking. It is well to cultivate faith and hope, but also most unwise to live under the delusion that every rich man appealed to would send his cheque by return of post. It may be very impolite of Mr. Carnegie not even to reply, but has not the bombarded millionaire some excuse when it is remembered he is the recipient of some five hundred letters - some very bulky and formidable - every day. They flow from all comers of the globe into one silent grave - the waste-paper basket. Not one in a thousand reaches Mr. Carnegie's hands. They are sifted by keen, watchful eyes, and the majority meet with the same cruel fate. It is certainly good for the paper trade, but troublesome for the secretaries, and mercilessly destructive to the fond hopes of the senders.

Mr. Carnegie concluded his article on "The Best Fields for Philanthropy" with the following impressive declaration: "The Gospel of Wealth but echoes Christ's words; it calls upon the millionaire to sell all he hath and give the highest and best to the poor, by administering his estate for his fellow men before he is called to lie down and rest upon the bosom of mother earth. So doing he will approach his end no longer the ignoble hoarder of useless millions; poor, very poor indeed in money, but rich, very rich in the affection, gratitude and admiration of his fellow men, and sweeter far, soothed and sustained by the still sweet voice within, which whispering tells him that because he has lived perhaps one small portion of the great world has been bettered just a little. This much is sure, against such riches as these no bar will be found at the gates of Paradise."

Mr. Carnegie has put before himself a noble and lofty ideal. His "Gospel of Wealth" found general acceptance. The world was amazed at its generous and liberal-hearted suggestions, and the spirit of unselfishness and practical charity which characterized it throughout. It was in many respects a unique manifesto, ably conceived, wisely arranged and strongly democratic in tone, and must be regarded as a valuable contribution to social scienc. Mr. Gladstone gave it his cordial approval and support, and a number of public men of all shades of thought were unanimous in their eulogy of its high tone and practical utility. The Pittsburgh millionaire leaped with one bound into the world's public arena and became one of the foremost and most discussed men on this side of the Atlantic and in America. It was one millionaire laying down the law for his brethren, a law which did not quite suit some tastes and inclinations. It was a bold attack upon miserly habits, selfish greed, and, of course, aroused some personal opposition and bitter criticism, but it was not without its good effect, and many wealthy men realized for the first time the great responsibilities attached to their riches.

Mr. Carnegie has not only theoretically discussed his "Gospel of Wealth" ; he has emphasized its utility by putting its principles into practice, and in this respect the future promises to be even richer in results than the past. This leads us to a consideration of his numerous gifts and benefactions.

Andrew Carnegie

CHAPTER X

HIS BENEFACTIONS

GIVING is at once the easiest and most difficult of arts. It is an art, because before proficiency can be attained much experience is necessary, and the judgment needs to have undergone a strict course of training. Liberality requires cultivation and care, like every other quality, and this more particularly applies to the man entrusted with millions of available wealth. It is somewhat of a paradox to find that wealth which has been amassed by conspicuous ability and hard toil is often distributed without discretion.

This cannot be said of Mr. Andrew Carnegie. He has acquired his wealth by the power of his brains, but he has not squandered his earnings by indiscriminate charity. There may be some dissent with his methods^ but general approval will be given to the munificent gifts he has made and the schemes he has financially launched. His aim has been to help the masses, and to encourage those who are striving by personal effort to cultivate their intellects and to improve their positions in the world. Self-help has been the motive power which has influenced most of his benefactions, and in this respect he has offered many splendid inducements to young men to climb the ladder of success by the rungs of education.

Up to June, 1902, Mr. Carnegie's benefactions amounted to nearly $100,000,000. This huge total is probably the largest aggregate of money given away by one man. It is really impossible accurately to estimate what the Pittsburgh millionaire has distributed in gifts during the past thirty years, but any estimate is likely to be under rather than above the mark.

Before he sailed for England in 1901 he left four letters announcing gifts amounting to $9,000,000. This munificent sum was made up of $4,000,000 to provide a pension fund for the workmen of the Carnegie Steel Company, $1,000,000 for the support of the libraries established for workmen at his works, $5,200,000 for the erection of sixty-five branch libraries in New York, and $1,000,000 to the city of St. Louis, Missouri, for a similar object. Although these four letters bore the same date, March 12, this does not signify that these magnificent gifts were hastily decided upon. The facts are just the reverse. These endowments were the result of careful inquiry, and had been under Mr. Carnegie's consideration for some time. Mr. Carnegie thinks before he gives, and often consults with intimate friends before he finally decides.

At the time of his departure from New York he said: "I have just begun to give away money," and based upon that assertion the future should reveal unparalleled gifts to an expectant world. One possessed of his great fortune has unlimited opportunities at his command and immeasurable responsibilities placed upon him. His position is unique, and without parallel in modem history. The world lies at his feet awaiting his endowments and wondering how he will fulfil his gospel.

The greater portion of the money Mr. Carnegie has given away so far has been for the erection of free libraries. This is the steel millionaire's favorite sphere. He firmly believes it contains the most prolific soil, and only needs developing to play an important part in the world's educational progress.

Speaking of circulating libraries he once said: "In all my experience I have never known so little produce such great, and as I believe, real beneficial and enduring results. I cannot but think it only needs to be known that the opportunity to do so much good is within the reach of wealthy men for so small a pittance from their store." His robust faith in the far-reaching results of well-equipped libraries is, like other strong convictions, the heritage of his boyhood. He has culled a leaf from his own life and applied it to the needs of the struggling poor and the respectable artisan, and it is from this source that his liberality in founding free libraries and public rooms has sprung.

When a boy in Pittsburgh, striving with all his might to improve his prospects, he was permitted with some other youths to borrow books from the library of a gentleman named Colonel Anderson. Every Saturday afternoon the good-hearted Colonel was in attendance at his house to lend any of his four hundred books. Young Carnegie eagerly looked forward to those Saturday afternoons. They were the sunny days of his youth, and the great joy they gave him has never faded from his memory. The opportunity of reading another book made the week swing along more smoothly. This privilege was shared by his brother Tom and his future partner, Mr. Phipps. The young telegraph messenger resolved in his buoyant enthusiasm that if ever wealth fell to his lot he would use it to establish free libraries, so that poor boys might have opportunities of reading the best books. His two companions little thought that Andrew's resolve would one day be realized, and that he would earn for himself a name as the greatest Mend free libraries have ever had since their birth. Mr. Carnegie holds the memory of

Colonel Anderson's kindly act in the deepest reverence, and it is as his disciple he has entered upon his labor of love in presenting libraries to those towns that will undertake efficiently to maintain them. There is an element of romance in this striking episode which gives to the task he has set himself an additional charm. It is a magnificent testimony to the far-reaching value of a thoughtful action, and teaches a significant lesson, especially to those who have it within their power to help boys to rise to positions of usualness.

Mr. Carnegie has made grants for the erection of more than 375 libraries in the United States alone, and the following among a large number of American towns have benefited by his generosity: New York, $5,200,000; Pittsburgh, $9,500,000 for Institute and Technical School; St. Louis, $1,000,000; Alleghany, $275,000; Braddock, $500,000; Washington, $10,350,000, including the Carnegie Institution; Johnstown, $50,000; Fairfield, $40,000; San Francisco, $750,000 ; Louisville, $250,000; Detroit, $750,000. The list of these gifts has now reached a magnificent total.

He has been nearly as liberal to the people of his native land, and has presented or aided free libraries in Edinburgh, Dunfermline, Aberdeen, Peterhead, Inverness, Ayr, Elgin, Wick and Kirkwall, and has contributed to the establishment of many public halls and reading-rooms in various other towns.

As an acknowledgment of his patriotic support he has been presented with the freedom of eleven towns of his native land, including the capital, a record of which he is justly proud. He greatly prizes these honors and the cordial welcome extended to him by his own countrymen.

This does not, however, complete the list of his gifts to Scottish libraries. He signalized his return to his native land in May, 1901, by making a handsome offer to the Corporation of Glasgow. The Lord Provost, who presided at a meeting of the city council on May 16th, announced that the following letter had been placed in his hands the previous day:

"My Dear Lord Provost : - It will give me pleasure to provide the needed £100,000 for Branch Libraries, which are sure to prove of great advantage to the masses of the people. It is just fifty years since my parents with their little boys sailed from Broomielaw for New York in the barque *Wiscassett*, 900 tons, and it is delightful to be permitted to commemorate the event upon my visit to you. Glasgow has done so much in municipal affairs to educate other cities, and to help herself, that it is a privilege to help her. Let

Glasgow flourish! So say all of us Scotsmen throughout the world. Always yours,

Andrew Carnegie."

Before we pass on to refer to his other benefactions, a description of the magnificent library he gave to Pittsburgh, the city of his commercial triumph, and those he presented to Allegheny and Braddock, will not be out of place; it will at least show how thoroughly Mr. Carnegie carries out his free library schemes, and the efficient manner in which he launches these educational instruments upon their careers.

The first library he endowed was the one at Braddock, a town of about 20,000 inhabitants, who are most of them employed at the Carnegie Steel Works. The library gradually outgrew its accommodation, and the formation of a Carnegie Club necessitated a large addition to the buildings. A new hall to seat 1,100 people was built, and a large gymnasium with a swimming bath was added. In addition to these a billiard-room was opened for the use of club members. The club proved a great success, the members paying an annual subscription of six shillings.

Soon afterward he offered to present to the neighboring town of Alleghany, at a cost of $375,000, a library with shelving accommodation for 70,000 volumes, a concert hall with a $10,000 organ, a lecture room, and an art gallery, providing the corporation found the site and the $15,000 per annum necessary to maintain it. The offer was accepted, and the buildings were formally opened by President Harrison on February 13, 1890. Four years after it had been opened the number of books in circulation was returned at 125,000 volumes, and it was estimated that 160,000 periodicals had been in use throughout the year. The government of the library is invested in a committee elected by the City Council.

The largest block of buildings Mr. Carnegie has erected is the vast fabric at Pittsburgh known as the Carnegie Institute. The name of Carnegie is indelibly associated with the great steel centre. He offered to provide $1,100,000 for free library buildings, on condition that the City Council agreed to spend annually on its maintenance and equipment $40,000, and that the management of the institution should be invested in a committee, half the members of which were to be nominated by himself, the other half by the Council. The offer at first was not accepted, but as the result of a popular agitation the sleepy Council were aroused to a sense of their duty, and after some maneuvering, during which Mr. Carnegie's playful humor was highly successful, he agreed to renew his offer.

The institute, which was opened in November, 1895, is a magnificent structure of gray sandstone in the Italian renaissance style of architecture. On the ground floor a spacious entrance hall leads to the circulating library and reading-rooms. On the second floor are located the main reference library and the stack-room with a capacity of 1 50,000 volumes. One portion of the building comprises a music hall, capable of seating 2,100 persons, and a stage for sixty musicians and a chorus of two hundred. It is enriched by a splendid pipe organ, on which every week a free organ recital is given. Mr. Carnegie borrowed the idea of giving free organ recitals from Birmingham, where for the first time he heard the city organist give a public recital. Another section of this vast block of imposing architecture is set aside as an art gallery and museum, and one wing of it supplies a spacious lecture hall and rooms for debating and scientific societies. In the basement are a number of classrooms, where instruction is given in various kinds of technical work. The building is illuminated throughout by electricity, and is fitted up with the most modern ventilating and heating apparatus. Connected with this library are seven distributing stations in the outlying districts. The institute has been used to a remarkable extent by the workmen in the iron and steel works for improving their knowledge and gaining technical information about their work. Special literature on engineering, natural philosophy and the useful arts is widely read. Two million dollars has also been given to establish a Polytechnic School in Pittsburgh. These magnificent gifts speak louder than words of Mr. Carnegie's interest in and affection for the city wherein his success was won. There are many evidences that these great gifts of Mr. Carnegie have proved an immense influence for good on the life of the city.

Next to his adopted country his native land has been the largest recipient of his generosity. Dunfermline, his birthplace, may almost be regarded as an endowed city. To Mr. Carnegie it owes its swimming baths, library and technical school - a building which was opened in October, 1899, and is a most practical seat of learning. It has fine spacious workshops, fitted with modern tools for instruction in wood-work, metal-work, mechanical engineering and mining, and also a physical laboratory; Special attention is given to local industries in the weaving department, which is equipped with two power looms and six hand looms.

England has so far participated but little in his lavish endowments. He, however, made an open offer to English-speaking towns in May, 1902. When he received the freedom of the city from the Guild of Plumbers in London, he stated in a speech that he stood ready to contribute toward the erection of a free library, provided the local authorities would spend not less than ten per cent, of his gift a year on its maintenance. This offer has already been taken advantage of in several instances, and as it becomes more widely known no doubt there will be an increasing number of applications. This was not done on the spur of the moment, but after deliberate study, and we may be sure he meant what he said.

MR. CARNEGIE'S NEW YORK HOME—FRONT VIEW

While the majority of Mr. Carnegie's larger gifts have thus been made to his adopted country and to his native land, there is one conspicuous exception - his donation of $250,000 to the endowment fund of the New Birmingham University. This handsome recognition of Birmingham's effort to establish in her midst a modem university, where her sons can receive an educational equipment to enable them to vie successfully with foreign competitors, was made through the Chancellor of the University, the Right Hon. Joseph Chamberlain, M. P., who, in communicating the offer to the Lord Mayor, wrote: ' 'I feel convinced that this munificent offer of Mr. Andrew Carnegie will be gratefully accepted by the promoters of the new university, and will be thoroughly appreciated by the people of Birmingham." Mr. Carnegie's unexpected assistance was heartily welcomed by the inhabitants of the Midland metropolis, whose feelings of deep gratitude were admirably reflected in the leading columns of the two principal morning papers, the Daily Post and the Daily Gazette. It not only gave a fresh impetus to the scheme, but aroused widespread interest throughout the country. His letter, which we have already produced, was made the theme of numerous articles in the daily press, and stirred up hopes that the gift was to be the forerunner of others of a similar nature. Mr. Carnegie's generosity is always preceded by careful consideration, and there is no reason to doubt that he repeat his offer to any other English city desirous of founding a modem university with a faculty of commerce as one of its distinguishing features.

Mr. Carnegie's munificent help put the Birmingham University scheme on the highroad to success. It drew attention to the need of such a seat of learning in a district where nearly the whole of the inhabitants are dependent upon manufactures and industrial pursuits, and also led to a movement being set on foot for the support of the scheme by employers of labor. To-day the Birmingham University is a reality, having received its charter and conferred its first degrees. Its endowment fund has reached the splendid total of $2,000,000, a result largely due to the strenuous efforts and personal influence of Mr. Joseph Chamberlain. As Mr. Carnegie views the progress this Midland University is making, and the sphere of usefulness it is aspiring to attain as a commercial power, he must feel thankful that he extended to it a helping hand. It promises to be one of his most fruitful gifts, and the future is sure to justify the wisdom of his decision and the thoughtful suggestions contained in his letter.

A noticeable feature of Mr. Carnegie's benefactions is, as already stated, the small amount he has given to strictly religious work. In his "Gospel of Wealth" he gave his reasons for this decision. He has no atheistic prejudice against Christian work, but he believes that those who hold a particular creed should render it pecuniary as well as moral assistance. The millionaire who appoints himself a trustee for the English-speaking race cannot, in justice to his position, favor one special denomination, as his bounden duty is to distribute his wealth so that all may derive some benefit. His aims must be cosmopolitan, and the channels through which his benefactions flow wide enough for the whole race to participate in. Such is Mr. Carnegie's conviction, and although many people may think that he is thus cutting himself off from a fruitful sphere, and that his attitude is too rigid, it does not seem probable that he will depart from his line of action. Although Mr. Carnegie has not given directly to the maintenance of religious work, he has presented churches with a great many organs. He is passionately fond of music, and, like many others, he can derive greater benefit from its fascinating and soul-stirring eloquence than from listening to scores of sermons. He once said he would hold himself responsible for what the organ pealed forth on the Sabbath, but not for what issued from the pulpit. It is this inherent love of music, and faith in its boundless power, which has induced him to subscribe toward the cost of church organs. The founding of a National School of Music has engaged his attention upon more than one occasion.

In 1891 he erected at a cost of $2,000,000 a magnificent concert hall in New York for the use of the general public. This hall, which is situated in Fifty-Seventh Street, will seat 3,000 persons. It is arranged on modem lines, and illuminated by 4,000 electric lights. It is one of the finest concert halls in the United States, and has been greatly appreciated by the public since it was opened. The donor of this magnificent hall enjoys holding the office of President of the New York Philharmonic Society, which has its offices in the great building.

We have already mentioned Mr. Carnegie's handsome endowment of $4,000,000 as a pension fund for the work-people of the Carnegie Steel Company. The object of this fund is to provide small pensions or aids to such employees as, after long and creditable service, through exceptional circumstances need such help in their old age, and who make a good use of it. It is intended to give aid to the injured, or to their families, or to employees who are needy in old age through no fault of their own, and to secure some provision against want as long as there is need, or until young children can become self-supporting. In his letter announcing the gift he said: "I make this first use of surplus wealth upon retiring from business as an acknowledgment of the deep debt which I owe to the workmen who have contributed so greatly to my success." Mr. Carnegie has set a splendid example, and one that is worthy of more general adoption by employers of labor in this country and in England.

And now we turn to review Mr. Carnegie's princely gift of two millions to Scottish University education. No man has a more ardent love for his native country than Andrew Carnegie has for Scotia's "Isle." Like every Scotchman, he has his own high estimate of the national virtues. The greatest compliment he could pay the American was to describe him as a "Scotchman with his coat off and his sleeves rolled up." Scotchmen, he firmly believes, are capable of doing anything human power can accomplish. Whether he considers them the superior of the American, which is perhaps an impossibility, or puts them both on the same level, is a doubtful point. Anyhow, he is never tired of singing their praises, and he has said that he is more thankful for being a Scotchman than for any other circumstance. In his opinion, no nation has more to be proud of than that which has for its heroes such men as Wallace, Bruce and Bums. It is not surprising, therefore, that he should honor Scotland with a great act of munificence. His patriotic benefaction was decided upon after careful deliberation and consultation with the principal educationalists in Scotland.

The source from which Mr. Carnegie drew his inspiration was an article which appeared some years ago in the *Nineteenth Century Review*, advocating free university education. The writer, Mr. Thomas Shaw, M. P., is also a native of Dunfermline, and has also made his own way in the world. The son of a baker, he rose by sheer merit to the position of Solicitor-General for Scotland in the last Liberal administration. This article attracted the attention of the Scottish-American millionaire, and the two Dunfermline men had many conversations about its main idea. After a lapse of a few years Mr. Carnegie has carried the principles of the scheme into practical effect, with an endowment of £2,000,000.

The preamble of the deed conveying the gift states that, having retired from active business, he deems it "to be his duty and one of his highest privileges to administer the wealth which has come to him as a trustee on behalf of others." Being fully convinced that one of the best means of discharging that trust is "by providing funds for improving and extending the opportunities for scientific study and research in the universities of Scotland, and by rendering attendance at these universities, and the enjoyment of their advantages, more available to the deserving and qualified youth of Scotland, to whom the payment of fees might act as a barrier to the enjoyment of these advantages," he decided to transfer to a body of trustees bonds of the United States Steel Corporation of the aggregate value of $10,000,000, bearing interest at five per cent, per annum, and having a currency of fifty years. The income to be derived from this endowment by the trustees will be therefore $500,000 per annum.

The trustees appointed include some of the foremost public men of the day, and it is worthy of note that they are all connected with Scotland, either by birth or by adoption, or as representatives of Scottish constituencies in the British Parliament, and that they comprise all shades of political thought.

The names of the trustees are the Earl of Elgin (chairman); the Earl of Rosebery; Lord Balfour of Burleigh; Lord Kelvin; Lord Reay; Lord Kinnear; Sir Henry Campbell-Bannerman, M. P.; Mr. A. J. Balfour, M. P.; Mr. Bryce, M. P.; Mr. John Morley, M. P.; Sir Robert Pullar; Sir Henry E. Roscoe; Mr. Haldane, M. P.; and Mr. Thomas Shaw, M. P. The following are trustees *ex officio*: The Secretary for Scotland; the Lords Provost of Edinburgh, Glasgow and Dunfermline. The four universities are each to be represented by one trustee, to be chosen by the University Courts. The trust deed is followed by a constitution, which provides that the administration of the trust shall be conducted by an executive committee of nine members. The first committee is constituted as follows: The Earl of Elgin (chairman), Lord Balfour of Burleigh, Lord Kinnear, Sir Henry E. Roscoe, Mr. Thomas

Shaw, the Lord Provost of Edinburgh, the Lord Provost of Glasgow. The two remaining members are to be two of the four trustees nominated by the University Courts, the members for Edinburgh and Aberdeen acting during the first two years and the members for Glasgow and St. Andrew acting during the second two years. The committee have full power and discretion in dealing with the income of the trust, and expending it in such a manner as they consider will best promote the interests of Scottish university education.

The trust deed states that one-half of the net annual income is to be applied toward the improvement and expansion of the universities of Scotland in the faculties of science and medicine, also for improving and extending the opportunities for scientific study and research, and for increasing the facilities for acquiring a knowledge of history, economics, English literature and modem languages, and such other subjects, cognate to a technical or commercial education, as can be brought within the scope of the university curriculum by the erection of buildings, laboratories, classrooms, museums or libraries; the provision of efficient apparatus, books and equipment; the institution and endowment of the professorships and lecture- ships, including post-graduate lectureships and scholarships, more especially scholarships for the purpose of encouraging research in any one or more of the subjects before named.

If it is found necessary the future income of the trust may be mortgaged to further the above objects, subject to the consent of the majority of the trustees being obtained.

The other half of the income, or such part thereof as in each year may be found requisite, is to be devoted to the payment of the whole or part of the ordinary class fees exacted by the universities from students of Scottish birth or extraction, and of sixteen years of age upward, or scholars who have given two years' attendance after the age of fourteen years at State-aided schools in Scotland, or at such other schools and institutes in Scotland as are under the inspection of the Scottish Educational Department. The student must have passed in the subject-matter of the class in which payment of fees is desired an examination qualifying for admission to the study of that subject at the universities with a view to graduation in any of the faculties. The students are to make application for the payment of their fees in such form as may be prescribed by the committee. The decision of the committee in all questions of qualification is to be final, and the fees of all applicants declared to be eligible are in each case to be paid by the committee as they become due to the factors or authorized officers of the universities.

If the committee, after due inquiry, are satisfied that any student has shown exceptional merit at the university, and may advantageously be afforded assistance beyond the payment of ordinary class fees, they are to have power to extend such assistance either in money or other privileges, upon such conditions and under such regulations as they may prescribe. They are to have power to withhold payment of fees from any student who is guilty of misconduct, or who fails within a reasonable time to pass the ordinary examination of the universities, or any of them.

Extra mural colleges, science schools or evening classes in Scotland, attendance at which is recognized as qualifying or assisting to qualify for graduation, are entitled to participate in any surplus income. The committee are also authorized to expend any unused income in establishing courses of lectures for the benefit of evening classes, attended by students engaged in industrial or professional occupation during the day, or in any other way they think proper in connection with the purposes expressed in the trust deed and constitution. In the event of the full income not being expended, the balance is to be paid into a reserve fund. The benefits of the trust are available to students of both sexes. The trustees have power by a two-thirds majority to modify the conditions under which the funds may be applied to meet the purposes of the donor, as expressed in the constitution, and according to the changed conditions of the time. Mr. Carnegie signed the trust deed on June 7, 1901, from which date the benefits accruing from his magnificent gift began to operate.

The publication of the details of the scheme attracted widespread attention. The inevitable faint rumblings of the critics were heard, but generally the scheme was heartily approved. A certain few, who had not grasped the comprehensive nature of the trust, asserted that it would pauperize University education and lower its dignity, but this result will be impossible if the stipulations contained in the trust deed are carried out. The scheme aims at opening the portals of University education to those of Scotland's sons and daughters who show evidences of maturing abilities and a desire to cultivate their gifts and extend their knowledge. Scotland need not trouble itself about the class of intellectual paupers free university education will produce, for they are destined to occupy the great positions of their land and to form the solid foundation of its commercial prosperity.

Mr. Carnegie has given instructions that the self-respect of parents and students should be recognized. Provision will be made for treating the sums paid for fees as advances to be repaid or not at the recipient's choice. He believes some of the truest and best will one day, if ever they become rich, remember the trust which gave them educational assistance in the days of industrious poverty. The proceedings of the trustees will be strictly confidential, and it will therefore not be known whether or not a student has paid any fees.

Speaking at the time when the scheme was made public, both Sir Henry Campbell-Bannerman and Mr. John Morley made appreciative references to Mr. Carnegie's unique offer. The Times, however, went so far as to express the hope that the non-payment of fees would eventually be abolished, in order that all the money could be devoted to "providing world-renowned laboratories of science." This view found scant favor, especially among Mr. Carnegie's countrymen, who recognized that he had already made provision for research, and that the primary object of his great scheme was not to improve the lot of the professor, but to aid and stimulate the industrious student with slender means and high aspirations.

As the scheme became more generally understood, and hasty and imperfect conception gave place to deliberate examination, the wisdom and foresight of the founder was conceded by even the critics, and it was frankly acknowledged that by his princely endowment Mr. Carnegie was giving the youth of Scotland the best and surest equipment to enable them successfully to meet commercial and professional competition. In future years thousands of Scotchmen will bless the name of Carnegie and honor the man whose patriotic action placed within their reach the highest education. A generation hence the foremost men in Britain will bear grateful testimony to Mr. Carnegie as the benefactor who made it possible for them to lay the foundation of a successful career by assisting them to obtain a thorough education.

Following closely the announcement of the details of the great gift to the Scottish universities came the rumor of a similar gift to the people of the United States. Washington, the centre of government of the Republic of which Andrew Carnegie is so loyal and eminent a citizen, is the seat of the Carnegie Institution. This great gift of $10,000,000 is parallel in many ways with the gift to the Scottish universities, as will be seen by the informal plan of the Carnegie Institution, prepared by Dr. Daniel C. Gilman.

Among its aims are these:

To increase the efficiency of the universities and other institutions of learning throughout the country, by seeking to utilize and add to their existing facilities, and to aid teachers in the various institutions for experimental and other work in these institutions as far as practicable.

To discover the invaluable and exceptional man in every department of study, whenever and wherever found, inside or outside of the schools, and enable him by financial aid to make the work for which he seems specially designed his life-work.

To promote original research, paying great attention thereto, as being one of the chief purposes of this institution.

To increase facilities for higher education.

To make more useful, to such students as may find Washington the best point for their special studies, the museums, libraries, laboratories, observatory, meteorological, piscicultural and forestry schools, and kindred institutions of the several departments of the government.

To insure the prompt publication and distribution of the results of scientific investigation, a field considered to be highly important.

These and kindred objects are to be attained by the employment of able teachers in the various institutions in Washington, or at other points, and by enabling men fitted for special work to devote themselves to it, through salaried fellowships or scholarships, or through salaries carrying pensions in old age, or through aid in other forms to such men as continue their special work at seats of learning, or who may be discovered outside the schools.

The form of organization is very simple. Under the general law of the District of Columbia six persons - namely, Messrs. John Hay, Edward D. White, John S. Billings, Charles D. Walcott, Carroll D. Wright and Daniel C. Oilman - formed an incorporation at Mr. Carnegie's request, and subsequently, on his nomination, selected twenty-seven persons to be the trustees, namely: the President of the United States, the President of the United States Senate, the Speaker of the House of Representatives, the Secretary of the Smithsonian Institution, the President of the National Academy of Sciences, ex officiis; Grover Cleveland, John S. Billings, William N. Frey, Lyman J. Gage, Daniel C. Gilman, John Hay, Abram S. Hewitt, Henry L. Higginson, Henry Hitchcock, Charles L. Hutchinson, William Lindsay, Seth Low, Wayne MacVeagh, D. O, Mills, S. Weir Mitchell, W. W. Morrow, Elihu Root, John C. Spooner, Andrew D. White, Edward D. White, Charles D. Walcott and Carroll D. Wright.

Mr. Carnegie's gift made possible, but much more comprehensively, a great educational scheme that originated in the mind of George Washington and has been a dream of educators ever since.

Mr. Carnegie's chief aims in the distribution of his wealth, so far, have been to assist the spread of knowledge, to encourage self-help and industrious ambition, and to implant noble ideals of citizenship and brotherhood in the minds of the rising generation. Mr. Gladstone spoke of his methods of bestowal as being worthy of high praise, and said that their effect would be to "teach high thought and amiable words, and courtliness, and the desire of fame, and love of truth, and all that makes a man." This eulogy has already been well earned by its recipient.

CHAPTER XI

THE PEN OF A READY WRITER

LITERARY pursuits have always been to Andrew Carnegie a real source of pleasure He has allowed his natural gifts in this direction to have full scope, and has acquired a worthy reputation as a strong and incisive writer, with a vivid, attractive style and a mastery of powerful illustration and apt quotation.

Notwithstanding the heavy tax upon his time and energies involved in the building up of the gigantic concern which bears his name, he has found leisure to indulge in literary work. The journalistic craving has always been strong within him, and the writing of articles, chiefly on commercial, political and social questions, for the principal reviews of both countries, has been to him a welcome recreation from the storm and stress of business. We have already referred to the most important of his articles, which earned him his international notoriety as a writer and social reformer.

In addition to a large number of lengthy and valuable magazine articles, he has written four books. His first publication, entitled "Round the World," which appeared in 1879, contained a picturesque account of a trip across the Pacific to Japan, China and India, and home again via the Suez Canal and Europe. There is much in this book that shows the characteristics of the man, his keen estimate of German nature, his interest in and understanding of social and political economics. Many of Mr. Carnegie's descriptions are as graphic as they are unconventional. He has the following to say about the first sight of Japan and the landing:

"Land ahoy! The islands of Japan are in sight, and the entrance to the bay is reached at 4 p. m. The sail up this bay is never to be forgotten. The sun set as we entered, and then came such a sky as Italy cannot rival. I have seen it pictured as deluging Egypt with its glory, but this we have yet to see. Fusiyama itself shone forth under its rays, its very summit clear, more than 14,000 feet above us. The clouds in large masses lay east and west of the peak, but cowering far below, as if not one speck dared to rise to its crown. It stood alone in solitary grandeur, by far the most impressive mountain I have yet seen; for mountains, as a rule, are disappointing, the height being generally attained by gradations. It is only to Fusiyama, and such as it, that rise alone in one unbroken pyramid, that one can apply Schiller's grand line,

"Ye are the things which tower."

Fusiyama *towers* beyond any crag or peak I know of, and I do not wonder that in early days the Japanese made the home of their gods upon its crest.

"It was nine o'clock when the anchor dropped, and in a few minutes after small boats crowded alongside to take us ashore. Until you are rowed in a sampan in style, never flatter yourself you have known the grotesque in the way of transportation. Fancy a large, wide canoe, with a small cabin in the stem, the deck in front lower than the sides, and on this four creatures, resembling nothing on earth so much as the demons in the Black Crook, minus most of the covering. They stand two on each side, but not in a line, and each works a long oar scull-fashion, accompanying each stroke with shouts such as we have never heard before ; the last one steers as well as sculls with his oar, and thus we go, propelled by these yelling devils, who apparently work themselves into a state of fearful excitement."

This paragraph, written as the author is about to leave the land of the Rising Sun, contains a prophecy that has long been realized:

"That Japan will succeed in her effort to establish a central government under something like our ideas of freedom and law, and that she has such resources as will enable her to maintain it and educate her people I am glad to be able to say I believe; but much remains to be done requiring in the race the exercise of solid qualities, the possession of which I find some Europeans disposed to deny them. They have traveled, perhaps, quite fast enough, and I look for a temporary triumph of the more conservative party. But the seed is sown, and Japan will move, upon the whole, in the direction of progress.'

Referring to the conditions in Ceylon, Mr. Carnegie has to say:

"I am amused at the ignorance of the average Englishman or American upon Eastern affairs. He is always amazed when I tell him that so far as representative institutions are concerned, there is not a village in India which is not further advanced in this department of politics than any rural constituency in Britain. The American county, village, district and township system is, of course, more perfect than any other with which I am acquainted, but the English is really about the most backward. The experiment in Ceylon of restoring the native system has been an unequivocal success, even beyond the expectations of its warmest advocates, and in addition to the advantages flowing from the native courts, it is found that the village committees are beginning to repair and restore the ancient tanks and other irrigation works, which, under the curse of centralized and foreign authority, had been allowed to fall into disuse."

The following passage is an interesting parallel to that quoting the wages of workingmen in England. The "land" referred to is India, and the place Benares.

"We are in the land of the cheapest labor in the world. It is doubtful if men can be found anywhere else to do a day's work for as little as they are paid in India. Railway laborers and coolies of all kinds receive only four rupees per month, and find themselves; these are worth just now forty cents each, or say $1.60 (6s. 6d.) in gold for a month's service. Upon this a man has to exist. Is it any wonder that the masses are constantly upon the verge of starvation? Women earn much less, and of course every member of a family has to work and earn something. The common food is a pulse called gran; the better class indulge in a pea called daahl. Anything beyond a vegetable diet is not dreamed of."

Mr. Carnegie's anti-imperialism crops out strongly in the following, but one cannot help thinking what a splendid thing England is doing in "giving to these millions the blessings of order" - well worth the cost.

"What do I think of India? is asked me every day; but I feel that one accustomed to the exceptional fertility and advantages of America â€" a land so wonderfully endowed that it seems to me more and more the special favorite of fortune â€" ^is very apt to underrate India. We saw it after two years of bad harvests and a third most unpromising one coming on. Judged from what I saw, I can only say that I, as a lover of England, find it impossible to repress the wish that springs up at every turn, Would she were safely and honorably out of it ? Retiring now is out of the question; she has abolished the native system in large districts, and must perforce continue the glorious task of giving to these millions the blessings of order."

This was followed in 1882 by "Our Coaching Trip," which is an interesting record of a drive on a coach and four through England and Scotland from Brighton to Inverness. These two books were intended for private circulation only, but they aroused so much interest that after giving away fifteen hundred copies of the latter work and a large number of the former a second issue of both was found necessary. "Our Coaching Trip" was re-entitled "An American Pour-in-Hand in Britain." Mr. Carnegie rambles on in a delightful way, digressing often, following any byway that might strike his fancy, stating facts, quoting appropriately at times.

Even in this lighter literature Mr. Carnegie's strong likes and dislikes show clearly; his abhorrence of war, his dislike for monarchical institutions, his: non-sectarianism all these characteristics crop out anywhere and everywhere.

A few quotations follow. Anent a visit to Parliament he says :

"The daily routine is uninteresting, and one sees how rapidly all houses of legislation are losing their hold upon public attention. A debate upon the propriety of allowing Manchester to dispose of her sewage to please herself, or of permitting Dunfermline to bring in a supply of water, seems such a waste of time. The Imperial Parliament of Great Britain is much in want of something to do when it condescends to occupy its time with trifling questions which the community interested can best settle; but even in matters of national importance debates are no longer what they were. The questions have already been threshed out in the Reviews - those coming forums of discussion - and all that can be said is already said by writers upon both sides of the question who know its bearings much better than the leaders of party."

The author's love for his adopted country rings out in the following:

"Do you know why the American worships the starry banner with a more intense passion than even the Briton does his flag? I will tell you. It is because it is not the flag of a government which discriminates between her children, decreeing privilege to one and denying it to another, but the flag of the people which gives the same rights to all. The British flag was born too soon to be close to the masses. It came before their time, when they had little or no power. They were not consulted about it. Some conclave made it, as a pope is made, and handed it down to the nation. But the American flag bears in every fiber the warrant, 'We the People in Congress assembled.' It is their own child, and how supremely it is beloved!"

And again in reference to Garfield:

"Garfield's life was not in vain. It tells it own story - this poor boy toiling upward to the proudest position on earth, the elected of fifty millions of freemen; a position compared with which that of king or kaiser is as nothing. Let other nations ask themselves where are our Lincolns and Garfields? Ah, they grow not except where all men are born equal! The cold shade of aristocracy nips them in the bud."

MR. CARNEGIE'S NEW YORK HOME, SHOWING THE GARDEN

He painted many pictures of English rural life and showed a surprising appreciation of Nature. Here is an illustration:

"The approach to Guilldford gives us our first real perfect English lane - so narrow and so bound in by towering hedgerows worthy the name. Had we met a vehicle at some of the prettiest turns there would have been trouble, for, although the lane is not quite as narrow as the pathway of the auld brig, where two wheelbarrows trembled as they met, yet a four-in-hand upon an English lane requires a clear tack. Vegetation near Guildford is luxuriant enough to meet our expectations of England. It was at the White Lion we halted, and here came our first experience of quarters for the night. The first dinner *en route* was a decided success in our fine sitting-room, the American flags, brought into requisition for the first time to decorate the mantel, bringing to all sweet memories of home. During our stroll to-day we stopped at a small village inn before which pretty roses grew, hanging in clusters upon its sides. It was a very small and humble inn indeed, the tile floors sanded, and the furniture of the tap-room only plain wood - there were no chairs, only benches around the table where the hinds sit at night, drinking home-brewed beer, smoking their day pipes, and discussing not the political affairs of the nation, but the affairs of their little world, bounded by the hall at one end of the estate and the parsonage at the other."

Also this bit of description:

"The rugs were laid under a chestnut tree, and our first picnic luncheon spread on the buttercups and daisies. Swallows skimmed the water, bees hummed above us - but stop! what's that, and where? Our first skylark singing at heaven's gate? All who heard this never-to-be-forgotten song for the first time were up and on their feet in an instant; but the tiny songster which was then filling the azure vault with music was nowhere to be seen. It's worth an Atlantic voyage to hear a skylark for the first time. Even luncheon was neglected awhile, hungry as we were, that we might if possible catch a glimpse of the warbler. The flood of song poured forth as we stood rapt awaiting the descent of the messenger from heaven. At last a small black speck came into sight. He is so little to see - so great to hear?

Interested in workmen the world over, Mr. Carnegie wormed the following from a carpenter whom he happened to meet:

"He was a rough carpenter and his wages were sixteen shillings per week ($4). A laborer gets eleven shillings (not $2.75), but some 'good masters' pay thirteen to fourteen shillings ($3.25 to $3.50) and give their men four or five pounds of beef at Christmas. Food is bacon and tea, which are cheap, but no beef. Men's wages have not advanced much for many years (I should think not !) , but women's have. An ordinary woman for field work can get one shilling per day (twenty-four cents); a short time ago ninepence (eighteen cents) was the highest amount paid. Is it not cheering to find poor women getting an advance? But think what their condition still is, when one shilling per day is considered good pay? I asked whether employers did not board the workers in addition to paying these wages, but he assured me they did not. This is Southern England and these are agricultural laborers, but the wages seem distressingly low even as compared with British wages in general. The new system of education and the coming extension of the suffrage to the counties will soon work a change among these poor people. They will not rest content crowding each other down thus to a pittance when they can read and write and vote. Thank fortune for this."

The following good advice Mr. Carnegie has followed himself. It is rather characteristic of the man that his preaching and his practice coincide:

"We strolled over and watched the cricketers. It all depends upon how you look at a thing. So many able-bodied perspiring men knocking about a little ball on a warm summer's day, that is one way; so many men relieved from anxious care and laying the foundations for long years of robust health by invigorating exercise in the open air, that is the other view of the question. The ancients did not count against our little time of life the days spent in the chase; neither need we charge those spent in cricket; and as for our sport, coaching, for every day so spent we decided that it and another might be safely credited. He was a very wise prime minister who said he had often found important duties for which he had not time; one duty, however, he had always made time for, his daily after- noon ride on horseback. Your always busy man accomplishes little; the great doer is he who has plenty of leisure. The man at the helm turns the wheel now and then, and so easily, too, touching an electric bell; it's the stoker down below who is pitching into it with his coat off. And look at Captain McMicken promenading the deck in his uniform and a face like a full moon; quite at his ease and ready for a story. And there is Johnnie Watson, chief engineer, who rules over the throbbing heart of the ship; he is standing there prepared for a crack. Moral: Don't worry yourself over work, hold yourself in reserve, and sure as fate 'it will all come right in the wash."

"A beautiful tribute to the mother land is found in the names of towns and cities in the new. As even on the crowded, tiny *Mayflower* the stern Puritan found room to bring and nurse with tender care the daisy of his native land, so the citizen, driven from the dear old home, ever sighs, 'England, with all thy faults I love thee still.' Surely, why not? Her faults are as one, her virtues as a thousand. And having a new home to christen, with swelling heart and tearful eye, and a love for the native land which knows no end and never can know end while breath clings to the body, he conjures up the object of his fondest love and calls his new home Boston, York, Brighton, Hartford, Stratford, Lynn, Liverpool, Glasgow, Edinburgh, Durham, Perth, Aberdeen, Dundee, Norwich, Cambridge, Oxford, Canterbury, Rochester, London, Newcastle, Manchester, Birmingham, Middleboro', Chester, Coventry, Plymouth, or other dear name of the place where in life's young days he had danced o'er the sunny braes, heard the lark sing in the heavens, and the mavis pour forth its glad song from the hedgerow. The Briton travels through the Republic living in a succession of hotels: Victorias, Clarendons, Windsors, Westminsters, Albemarles. He might think himself at home again except that the superior advantages of the new hostelries serve to remind him at every turn that things are not as he has been accustomed to. So that our household gods are not only the same in the new as in the old land, but we call them by the same names and love them. And what American worthy of the name but shall reverence the home of his fathers and wish it god speed? When the people reign in the old home as they do in the new, the two nations will become one people, and the bonds which unite them the world combined shall not break asunder. The republican on this side of the Atlantic will extend his hand to his fellow upon the other, and resolve that no difference between them shall ever lead to war. All parties in the Republic already stand pledged to the doctrine of peaceful arbitration. The reign of the masses is the road to universal peace. Thrones and royal families, and the influences necessarily surrounding jealous dynasties, make for war; the influences surrounding Democracy make for peace."

Andrew Carnegie the Scotchman describes himself when the border line was crossed and the coach entered Scotland:

"It was on Saturday, July 16th, that we went over the border. The bridge across the boundary line was soon reached. When midway over, a halt was called and vent given to our enthusiasm. With three cheers for the land of the heather, shouts of 'Scotland forever,' and the waving of hats and handkerchiefs, we dashed across the border. O Scotland, my own, my native land, your exiled son returns with love for you as ardent as ever warmed the heart of man for his country. It's a God's mercy I was born a Scotchman, for I do not see how I could ever have been contented to be anything else. The little plucky dour deevil, set in her own ways and getting them, too, level-headed and shrewd, with an eye to the main chance always, and yet so lovingly weak, so fond, so led away by song or story, so easily touched to fine issues, so leal, so true! Ah, you suit me, Scotia, and proud am I that I am your son."

Altogether "An American Four-in-Hand in Britain" is an extremely vivacious book, sparkling with humor and gems of scenic description and chatty reminiscences.

In 1886 was published his best-known work, "Triumphant Democracy." The dedication of the book reads as follows – "To the beloved Republic, under whose equal laws I am made the peer of any man, although denied political equality by my native land, I dedicate this book, with an intensity of gratitude and admiration which the native-born citizen can neither feel nor understand." This, together with the first paragraph, indicates the trend of the book - "The old nations creep on at a snail's pace; the Republic thunders past with the rush of an express. The United States, the growth of a single century, has already reached the foremost rank among nations, and is destined soon to outdistance all others in the race. In population, in wealth, in annual savings, and in public credit; in freedom from debt, in agriculture and in manufactures America already leads the civilized world." At the time he wrote the book Mr. Carnegie was at the height of his political enthusiasm, and his caustic attacks on royalty and the aristocracy, together with the real merit of the volume in other respects, attracted a great deal of attention and criticism and aroused not a little righteous indignation.

With an enthusiasm for his adopted country that is splendid, and from the point of view of the Americanized Briton, he proceeds to tell the Republic's greatness.

"The American is tolerant. Politics do not divide people. Once in four years he warms up and takes sides, opposing hosts confront each other, and a stranger would naturally think that only violence could result whichever side won. The morning after election his arm is upon his opponent's shoulder and they are chaffing each other. All becomes as calm as a Summer sea. He fights "rebels" for four years, and as soon as they lay down their arms invites them to his banquets."

As to the question of the maintenance of the purely American race he has this to say:

"It is not unusual to find in the writings of Europeans statements to the effect that the American race is unable to maintain itself without the constant influx of foreign immigration. A position more directly opposed to the facts could scarcely be taken. Let us see. The total number of persons of foreign birth in the United States in 1890 was approximately 9,250,000. The total number of persons of native birth, but whose parents were of foreign birth, in 1890 was approximately 10,400,000. Now, since immigration on a large scale commenced at a comparatively recent date, it is not probable that there is any considerable number of persons of foreign parentage in the second generation. Therefore, the sum of these 19,650,000 or, in round numbers, 20,000,000, is probably a close approximation to the number of persons in the country of foreign birth or of foreign parentage.

THE PEN OF A READY WRITER 197

The number of whites in the United States in 1890 was, in round numbers, 55,000,000. Subtracting from this the above 20,000,000, leaves as the number of whites of native abstraction in the United States in 1890, 35,000,000. In 1840 the corresponding number was approximately 14,000,000, showing that in fifty years the native population, unaided by immigration, has much more than doubled - indeed, has increased no less than one hundred and fifty per cent. It does not look as if the 'American race' is not able to maintain itself."

For even the much maligned immigrant to the United States he has a good word:

"But the value of these peaceful invaders does not consist solely in their numbers or in the wealth which they bring. To estimate them aright we must take into consideration their superior character. As the people who laid the foundation of the American Republic were extremists, fanatics, if you will - men of advanced views intellectually, morally and politically; men whom Europe had rejected as dangerous - so the emigrants to-day are men who leave their native land from dissatisfaction with their surroundings, and who seek here, under new conditions, the opportunity for development denied them at home. The old and destitute, the idle and the contented, do not brave the waves of the stormy Atlantic, but sit hopelessly at home perhaps bewailing their hard fate, or, what is still more sad to see, aimlessly contented with it. The emigrant is the capable, energetic, ambitious, discontented man - who, longing to breathe the air of equality, resolves to tear himself away from the old home with its associations, to found in hospitable America a new home under equal and just laws, which insure to him, and - what counts with him and his wife far more - insure to their children the full measure of citizenship, making them free men in a free State, possessed of every right and privilege."

Mr. Carnegie, a thorough student of economics and prone to look well before he leaps, has no patience with snapshot legislation.

"These grand, immutable, all-wise laws of natural forces, how perfectly they work if human legislators would only let them alone! But no, they must be tinkering. One day they would protect the balance of power in Europe by keeping weak, small areas apart and independent - an impossible task, for petty States must merge into the greater: political is as certain as physical gravitation ; the next day it is silver in America which our sage rulers would make of greater intrinsic value. So our governors, all over the world, are at Sisyphus's work - ever rolling the stone uphill to see it roll back into its proper bed at the bottom."

Though Mr. Carnegie's enthusiasm for America and her institutions is one of his strongest feelings, he has a love for his mother country that crops out everywhere and tinges all his writings.

A hard worker himself, Mr. Carnegie thoroughly believes in the dignity of labor. The following paragraph from the chapter in 'Triumphant Democracy" on "Occupations" shows the importance he attaches to the American's capacity for work:

"There is still little realized wealth and only a trace of a leisure class. The climate stimulates to exertion. The opinion is very generally held that every citizen owes the Republic a life of usefulness. Carlyle says: 'Happy is the man who has found his work.' Very few Americans, indeed, are permitted to trace their unhappiness, if unhappiness there be, to a failure in this direction. Every man appears to have found his work and to be doing it with a will. The American likes work. He has not yet learned to play the idler gracefully. Even when old age appears he seems to find it more difficult than the man of any other race to retire from active and engrossing pursuits."

With Mr. Carnegie practice and preaching go hand in hand to a remarkable degree. The following paragraph from "Triumphant Democracy" matches the ten-million gifts for education in America and Scotland:

"The moral to be drawn from America by every nation is this: 'Seek ye first the education of the people, and all other political blessings will be added unto you.' The quarrels of party, the game of politics, this or that measure of reform, are but surface affairs of little moment. The education of the people is the real underlying work for earnest men who would best serve their country. In this, the most creditable work of all, it cannot be denied that the Republic occupies the first place."

The two following quotations contain the gist of Andrew Carnegie's feeling about churches and religious services:

One hundred and fifty differing sects are found in the United States, each fortunately certain that it has in its bosom the truth; and each has part of the truth. All truth is not to be gathered in one or all the sects. It is too vast, too all-pervading, to be cabined, cribbed, confined. As well might one country claim a monopoly of all the air of heaven, as one sect all the truth of heaven. Each may have some, but none can have all.

"Without church-rate or tithe, without State endowment or State supervision, religion in America has spontaneously acquired a strength which no political support could have given. It is a living force entering into the lives of the people, and drawing them closer together in unity of feeling, and working silently and without sign of friction which in the mother country results from a union with the State, which, as we have seen, tends strongly to keep the people divided one from another. The power of the church in America must not be sought, as Burke said of an ideal aristocracy, 'in rotten parchments, under dripping and perishing walls, but in full vigor, and acting with vital energy and power, in the character of the leading men and natural interests of the country.' Even if judged by the accommodations provided, and the sums spent upon church organizations, Democracy can safely claim that of all the divisions of English-speaking people, it has produced the most religious community yet known."

Commerce is a word spelled large in Mr. Carnegie's vocabulary - commercial success is much more to be honored than military glory - the man who achieves great things industrially is "greater than he who taketh a city" by force of arms.

"The United States of America probably furnish the only example in the world's history of a community purely industrial in origin and development. Every other nation seems to have passed through the military stage. In Europe and in Asia, in ancient times as well as in modem, social development has been mainly the result of war. Nearly every modem dynasty in Europe has been established by conquest, and every nation there has acquired and held its territory by force of arms. Men have been as wild beasts slaughtering each other at the command of the small privileged classes. The colonies of America, on the other hand, were established upon a peaceful basis, and the land chiefly obtained by purchase or agreement, and not by conquest. Devoted to industry, the American people have never taken up the sword except in self-defense or in defense of their institutions."

"Triumphant Democracy" reached a circulation of 40,000 copies in the first two years, and it acquired an added notoriety through the efforts of some superlatively loyal persons to have it suppressed.

Mr. Carnegie has published a dozen of his articles under the general title of "The Gospel of Wealth," and several of them have a direct bearing on the chief chapter. One of the most striking arguments in the "Gospel" is his contention that poverty is a positive help in the formation of character and the winning of success. The following passage is quoted from the above-mentioned book from "The Advantages of Poverty":

"Hereditary wealth and position tend to rob father and mother of their children and the children of father and mother. It cannot be long ere their disadvantages are felt more and more and the advantages of plain and simple living more clearly seen.

"Poor boys reared thus directly by their parents possess such advantages over those watched and taught by hired strangers, and exposed to the temptations of wealth and position, that it is not surprising they become the leaders in every branch of human action. They appear upon the stage, athletes trained for the contest, with sinews braced, indomitable wills, resolved to do or die. Such boys always have marched, and always will march, straight to the front and lead the world; they are the epoch-makers. Let one select the three or four foremost names, the supremely great in every field of human triumph, and note how small is the contribution of hereditary rank and wealth to the short list of the immortals who have lifted and advanced the race. It will, I think, be seen that the possession of these is almost fatal to greatness and goodness, and that the greatest and the best of our race have necessarily been nurtured in the bracing school of poverty - the only school capable of producing the supremely great, the genius."

Mr. Carnegie's ideas about trusts aroused a great deal of interest. He contends in general that trusts are inevitable and many of them distinctly beneficial to the public. The following quotation is from "Popular Illusions About Trusts":

"If there be in human history one truth clearer and more indisputable than another, it is that the cheapening of articles, whether of luxury or of necessity or of those classed as artistic, insures their more general distribution, and is one of the most potent factors in refining and lifting a people and in adding to its happiness. In no period of human activity has this great agency been so potent or so widespread as in our own.
Now, the cheapening of all these good things, whether it be the metals, in textiles or in food, or especially in books and prints, is rendered possible only through the operation of the law, which may be stated thus: cheapness is in proportion to the scale of production. To make ten tons of steel a day would cost many times as much per ton as to make one hundred tons; to make one hundred tons would cost double as much per ton as a thousand; and to make one thousand tons per day would cost greatly more than to make ten thousand tons. Thus, the larger the scale of operation the cheaper the product. The huge steamship of twenty thousand tons' burden carries its ton of freight at less cost, it is stated, than the first steamships carried a pound. It is, fortunately, impossible for man to impede, much less to

change, this great and beneficent law, from which flow most of his comforts and luxuries, and also most of the best and most improving forces in his life.

"In an age noted for its inventions we see the same law running through these. Inventions facilitate big operations, and in most instances, required to be worked upon a great scale. Indeed, as a rule, the great invention which is beneficent in its operation would be useless unless operated to supply a thousand people where ten were supplied before. Every agency in our day labors to scatter the good things of life, both for mind and body, among the toiling millions. Eyerywhere we look we see the inexorable law ever producing bigger and bigger things. One of the most notable illustrations of this is seen in the railway freight car. When the writer entered the service of the Pennsylvania Railroad from seven to eight tons were carried upon eight wheels ; to-day they carry fifty tons. The locomotive has quadrupled in power. The steamship to-day is ten times bigger, the blast-furnace has seven times more capacity, and the tendency everywhere is still to increase. The contrast between the hand printing press of old and the elaborate newspaper printing machine of to-day is even more marked."

Mr. Carnegie has to say of the relations of employer and employee as follows:

"It is the chairman, situated hundreds of miles away from his men, who only pays a flying visit to the works and perhaps finds time to walk through the mill or mine once or twice a year, that is chiefly responsible for the disputes which break out at intervals. I have noted that the manager who confers oftenest with a committee of his leading men has the least trouble with his workmen. Although it may be impracticable for the presidents of these large corporations to know the workingmen personally, the manager at the mills, having a committee of his best men to present their suggestions and wishes from time to time, can do much to maintain and strengthen amicable relations, if not interfered with from headquarters. I, therefore, recognize in trades unions, or better still, in the organizations of the men in each establishment, who select representatives to speak for them, a means, not of further embittering the relations between employer and employed, but of improving them."

Mr. Carnegie's latest book, "The Empire of Business," may be called a book of inspiration; it has a distinctly optimistic tone, and almost every chapter expresses the hopeful, cheerful disposition which is characteristic of its author. In this latest book Mr. Carnegie's well-known opinions about the uses of wealth, the advantages of poverty and the relations of capital and labor are clearly expressed. Beside these subjects Mr. Carnegie writes interestingly about such things as steel manufacture, oil and gas wells, and railroads, about which he is a recognized authority.

In "The A B C of Money" Mr. Carnegie has given a remarkably clear idea of the whole money question. The following gives the reason for money in a nutshell.

"To get at the root of the subject you must know, first, why money exists; secondly, what money really is. Let me try to tell you, taking a new district of our own modem country to illustrate how 'money' comes. In times past, when the people only tilled the soil, and commerce and manufactures had not developed, men had few wants, and so they got along without 'money' by exchanging the articles themselves when they needed something which they had not. The farmer who wanted a pair of shoes gave so many bushels of corn for them, and his wife bought her sun-bonnet by giving so many bushels of potatoes; thus all sales and purchases were made by exchanging articles - by barter.

"As population grew and wants extended, this plan became very inconvenient. One man in the district then started a general store and kept on hand a great many of the things which were most wanted, and took for these any of the articles which the farmer had to give in exchange. This was a great step in advance, for the farmer who wanted half a dozen different things when he went to the village had then no longer to search for half a dozen different people who wanted one or more of the things he had to offer in exchange. He could now go directly to one man, the storekeeper, and for any of his agricultural products he could get most of the articles he desired. It did not matter to the storekeeper whether he gave the farmer tea or coffee, blankets or a hayrake; nor did it matter what articles he took from the farmer, wheat or com or potatoes, so he could send them away to the city and get other articles for them which he wanted. The farmer could even pay the wages of his hired men by giving them orders for articles upon the store. No dollars appear here yet, you see; all is still barter - exchange of articles; very inconvenient and very costly, because the agricultural articles given in exchange had to be hauled about and were always changing their value."

The author stands for a gold standard, of course. He closes his article on the subject of money with the following earnest summing up :

"I have written in vain if this paper does not do something to explain why this is so, and to impel the people to let their representatives in Congress clearly understand that, come what may, the stamp of the republic must be made true, the money of the American people kept the highest and surest in value of all money in the world, above all doubt or suspicion, its standard in the future, as in the past, not fluctuating silver, but unchanging gold."

Andrew Carnegie has been called a "slave driver," and it has been said that his workmen have been driven unwarrantably. The facts in the case disprove this, and his writings show that he looked at things from the workman's point of view as well as that of the employer. The following quotations from two chapters of "The Empire of Business" show his attitude toward the question of capital and labor:

"It is very unfortunate that the irresistible tendency of our age, which draws manufacturing into immense establishments, requiring the work of thousands of men, renders it impossible for employers who reside near to obtain that intimate acquaintance with employers which, under the old system of manufacturing in very small establishments, made the relation of master and man more pleasing to both.

"When articles were manufactured in small shops by employers who required only the assistance of a few men and apprentices, the employer had opportunities to know every one, to become well acquainted with each, and to know his merits both as a man and as a workman; and on the other hand the workman, being brought into closer contact with his employer, inevitably knew more of his business, of his cares and troubles, of his efforts to succeed, and more important than all, they came to know something of the characteristics of the man himself. All this is changed.

"Thus the employes become more like human machines, as it were, to the employer, and the employer becomes almost a myth to his men. From every point of view this is a most regrettable result, yet it is one for which I see no remedy. The free play of economic laws is forcing the manufacture of all articles of general consumption more and more into the hands of a few enormous concerns, that their cost to the consumer may be less."

"It being therefore impossible for the employers of thousands to become acquainted with their men, if we are not to lose all feeling of mutuality between us, the employer must seek their acquaintance through other forms, to express his care for the well-being of those upon whose labor he depends for success, by devoting part of his earnings for institutions like this library, and for the accommodation of their organizations, and I hope in return that the employes are to show by the use which they make of such benefactions that they in turn respond to this sentiment upon the part of employers wherever it may be found.

"By such means as these we may hope to maintain to some extent the old feeling of kindliness, mutual confidence, respect and esteem which formerly distinguished the relations between the employer and his men."

"The great inventions, the improvements, the discoveries in science, the great works in literature have sprung from the ranks of the poor. You can scarcely name a great invention or a great discovery, you can scarcely name a great picture or a great statue, a great song or a great story, nor anything great, that has not been the product of men who started like yourselves to earn an honest living by honest work.

"And, believe me, the man whom the foreman does not appreciate, and the foreman whom the manager does not appreciate, and the manager whom the firm does not appreciate, has to find the fault not in the firm, or the manager, or the foreman, but in himself. He cannot give the service that which is so invaluable and so anxiously looked for. There is no man who may not rise to the highest position, nor is there any man who, from lack of the right qualities or failure to exercise them, may not sink to the lowest. Employes have chances to rise to higher work, to rise to foremen, to be superintendents, and even to rise to be partners, and even to be chairmen in our service, if they prove themselves possessed of the qualities required. They need never fear being dispensed with. It is we who fear that the abilities of such men may be lost to us."

The following from "The Three-Legged Stool" shows that Mr. Carnegie places labor on the same plane with capital and business ability.

"There is a partnership of three in the industrial world when an enterprise is planned. The first of these, not in importance but in time, is Capital. Without it nothing costly can be built. From it comes the first breath of life into matter, previously inert.

"The structures reared, equipped and ready to begin in any line of industrial activity, the second partner comes into operation. That is Business Ability. Capital has done its part. It has provided all the instrumentalities of production; but unless it can command the services of able men to manage the business, all that Capital has done crumbles into ruin.

"Then comes the third partner, last in order of time but not least, Labor. If it fails to perform its part, nothing can be accomplished. Capital and Business Ability, without it brought into play, are dead. The wheels cannot revolve unless the hand of Labor starts them.

"Now, volumes can be written as to which one of the three partners is first, second or third in importance, and the subject will remain just as it was before. Political economists, speculative philosophers and preachers have been giving their views on the subject for hundreds of years, but the answer has not yet been found, nor can it ever be, because each of the three is all-important, and everyone is equally essential to the other two. There is no first, second or last. There is no precedence! They are equal members of the great triple alliance which moves the industrial world. As a matter of history, Labor existed before Capital or Business Ability, for when 'Adam digged and Eve span ' Adam had no capital, and if one may judge from the sequel, neither of the two was inordinately blessed with business ability; but this was before the reign of Industrialism began and huge investments of Capital were necessary.

"In our day Capital, Business Ability, Manual Labor are the legs of a three-legged stool. While the three legs stand sound and firm, the stool stands; but let any one of the three weaken and break, let it be pulled out or struck out, down goes the stool to the ground. And the stool is of no use until the third leg is restored. "

The author of "The Gospel of Wealth" considers thrift an evidence of civilization : the following from his essay, "Thrift":

"The importance of the subject is suggested by the fact that the habit of thrift constitutes one of the greatest differences between the savage and the civilized man. One of the fundamental differences between savage and civilized life is the absence of thrift in the one and the presence of it in the other. When millions of men each save a little of their daily earnings, these petty sums combined make an enormous amount, which is called capital, about which so much is written. If men consumed each day of each week all they earned, as does the savage, of course there Would be no capital - that is, no savings laid up for future use.

Now, let us see what capital does in the world. We will consider what the shipbuilders do when they have to build great ships. These enterprising companies offer to build an ocean greyhound for, let us say, £500,000, to be paid only when the ship is delivered after satisfactory trial trips. Where or how do the shipbuilders get this sum of money to pay the workmen, the wood merchant, the steel manufacturer, and all the people who furnish material for the building of the ship? They get it from the savings of civilized men. It is part of the money saved for investment by the millions of industrious people. Each man, by thrift, saves a little, puts the money in a bank, and the bank lends it to the shipbuilders, who pay interest for the use of it. It is the same with the building of a manufactory, a railroad, a canal, or anything costly. We could not have had anything more than the savage had, except for thrift. "

Mr. Carnegie is an orator as well as an author. His speeches have a fine literary flavor, and are always distinguished by sound common-sense argument and logical reasoning. He is fertile in ideas and felicitous in expression, and speaks with a clear, telling voice, enforcing his points with graceful gesture.

CHAPTER XII

OBITER DICTA

I AM now entirely out of business, and nothing could tempt me to return." Mr. Carnegie had always intended to retire from business as soon after sixty as possible, and to spend the eventide of his life in "rest, recreation and philanthropy." The formation of the colossal Steel Trust, with a capital of $1,100,000,000, having afforded him the desired opportunity to dispose of his vast interests, the Steel King handed over his possessions, took up his $250,000,000 in five per cent, bonds and surplus before invested, and was free. The whole world was open to him, but he fulfilled universal expectations by electing to return to his native land and spend at least the summers of the remaining years of his life amongst the mountain and moor, and the heather and loch, of "Bonnie Scotland."

At the time when his father became a naturalized American Andrew was a minor, and consequently in due course he stepped into the rights and privileges, which he values so highly, of a full-fledged citizen of the United States. It is therefore only fitting that, as his country seat is in Scotland, his town residence should be in America. The palace on Fifth Avenue, New York, which he has built for his own use, is in all ways a dwelling-place worthy of a rich man. Mr. Carnegie, however, true to his democratic principles, gave instructions when the plans were being prepared that the chief consideration should be "beauty, simplicity and comfort." He recognized that his new residence, from its size and the extent of its grounds, must be a conspicuous object, but he deprecated unnecessary magnificence or useless display, and consequently his mansion is not so pretentious as many others in that city of millionaires. The material used in its construction was Indiana limestone and Harvard brick; the decorations are in marble, onyx and bronze. Mr. Carnegie will, no doubt, reside in New York during some portions of the year, but his absence from his beautiful retreat in the North of Scotland will not be of long duration. For many years he rented Cluny castle as his Scottish residence, but in 1895, hearing that Skibo castle was in the market, he instantly made inquiries about it, and was told that, although situated at the extreme North of Scotland, it enjoyed a beautiful climate, remarkably free from rawness, and exceedingly healthy.

He promptly secured the option to purchase it for $425,000, and was only just in time, as the trustees received three other offers a week later. In due course he entered into possession of his estate, and upon his arrival at his new home he met with an enthusiastic reception from the tenantry, who presented him with an address of welcome, and a flag bearing the inscription: "Presented to Andrew Carnegie, Esquire, by his tenants, crofters and feuars, on the occasion of his homecoming as the proprietor of Skibo." Mr. Carnegie made a characteristic reply, in which he said that this was his first experience of entering a large residential estate as its owner. The best title-deed to the land, and the best key to the castle, he added, would be the knowledge that he "possessed the hearts of his people."

Mr. Carnegie at once proceeded to overhaul the old castle, and drew up plans for comprehensive alterations. It was found necessary to demolish about half of it condemned as unsafe, and to make extensive alterations throughout. A new wing was added to provide more accommodation, the whole of the extensions and alterations being carried out on the most modern lines. The interior of the castle was entirely redecorated and refurnished, and a spacious library designed for the literary tastes of the new owner. The hall is of noble dimensions, and leading from it is a staircase of white Sicilian marble. The library contains 4,000 books.

The principal actor in the ceremony of laying the comer-stone of the new wing was Miss Margaret Carnegie, the owner's little daughter. In returning thanks for the gift of a trowel, with which the little maiden performed the ceremony, Mr. Carnegie said that "every year of his life confirmed him in the opinion that the greatest work men and women could perform was to establish on earth happy, virtuous, refined and earnest homes. The gift would be the most treasured heirloom of his daughter, and would teach her that any wealth and advantages that she might possess carried with them corresponding responsibilities." When his little girl was born the papers proclaimed her the heiress of millions. Commenting upon this report, Mr. Carnegie said, "My wife and daughter shall not be cursed with great wealth. Wealth can only bring happiness in the sense that it brings us greater opportunities of making others happy. The truest happiness is to make others happy." Mrs. Carnegie has herself no desire to inherit millions.

The fireside circle at Skibo is composed of Mr. Carnegie, his wife and daughter, and a sister of Mrs. Carnegie. The hostess is an American lady who has made herself beloved by all who have met her. Mrs. Carnegie who is twenty years younger than her husband, throws her heart and soul into all his schemes, and it is to her that he first turns for advice. She is consulted upon the management of his business affairs and public benefactions, and upon her womanly wisdom and far-seeing judgment his decision is often founded. Charming, vivacious and clever, Mrs. Carnegie is a model hostess, but she prefers to be regarded simply as the mistress of Skibo, and not as a person of public interest. She does not court the attention of the "personal paragraphist," and shuns that prying individual, "the interviewer."

Mr. Carnegie's home could not be otherwise than the centre of happiness, and it is made still more radiant with the joy of the presence of a sparkling jewel which is very dear to Mr. Carnegie's heart. When his little daughter was born Mr. Carnegie said he had now everything in the world his heart desired.

Skibo castle is situated on the northern shore of the Dornoch Firth, Sutherlandshire, in the midst of a romantic district, surrounded with a halo of tradition and teeming with innumerable legends. It has a high elevation, about half a mile from tidal water, and is sheltered from the northern winds by hills and woods, while from its windows a magnificent panorama of mountain and loch stretches southward. The grounds are extensive and beautifully laid out. The estate extends many miles inland from the firth, and includes hundreds of acres of brown heath and shaggy wood, over which Mr. Carnegie's guests enjoy as good grouse shooting as is to be found in Scotland.

In the park half a mile from the house lie the golf links, in which Mr. Carnegie takes such keen delight. During recent years they have been considerably developed and improved, until they are now one of the finest courses in the country. Mr. Carnegie is an enthusiast, and no mean exponent of the royal game. Every visitor to Skibo inspects the golf links, and nothing pleases the genial host more than for his guests to accompany him for a run over the long stretch of heather. He once said to a friend who was playing a game with him, and who had happened to make a long drive off the tee, that for the joy of making one such drive the payment of $10,000 would be cheap.

Mr. Carnegie is nearly as zealous in the pursuit of his other sport, but unlike most fishermen, he does not go simply to display his patience, for the streams he has resort to are filled with salmon and trout. The Laird of Skibo is also very fond of coaching, and by this means he has traveled many hundreds of miles both in Britain and America. A splendid sailor and an intense lover of the sea, he is never so happy as when being tossed in his beautifully equipped yacht, *The Seabreeze*, in which, when he is staying at Skibo, he takes frequent cruises. The frolics of King Neptune seem to harmonize with his nature and bring into play all his youthful spirits and enthusiasm. He says: 'To him who finds himself comfortable at sea, the ocean is the grandest of treats. He never fails to feel himself a boy again while on the waves. There is an exaltation about it. He walks the monarch of the peopled deck, glories in the storm, rises with it, and revels in it. Heroic song comes to him. The ship becomes a living thing, and if the monster rears and plunges it is akin to bounding on his thoroughbred who knows its rider. Many feel thus, and I am happily one of them."

Mr. Carnegie has a wide circle of friends, and many prominent public men have enjoyed the hospitality of Skibo since he became its owner. He is very proud of his Highland castle, which he once described as "his earthly paradise," and nothing gives him greater pleasure than to welcome his friends and point out to them the natural beauties of the surrounding district.

Mr. Carnegie is greatly respected by his tenants, who find in him an ideal landlord. He has instituted a number of reforms, and takes a deep interest in their home life and daily work. It is not an uncommon sight, when he is at Skibo, to see him engaged in a prolonged discussion with some old son of the soil, and he owns that he often emerges from the wordy conflict but "second best." From the old castle tower an immense double flag - the Union Jack and Stars and Stripes - floats in the breeze. A friend describing a visit he paid to Mr. Carnegie in his Highland home, says, "Mr. Carnegie keeps his own piper, and every morning the inmates are wakened by the shrill music of the Highlands. Before dinner the same bagpipes serve as the substitute for the dinner bell, and the piper marches to the dining-room, followed by the guests."

Life in Skibo resembles that in most Highland castles. The hall is littered with books and newspapers, both British and American, but a special feature is the organ, on which every morning before breakfast sweet music is discoursed. It is Mr. Carnegie's substitute for family prayers, and but the beginning of the musical service with which he hopes in time to salute each smiling mom.

In personal appearance Mr. Carnegie is a short, sprightly man, about five feet six inches in height, with an erect bearing, keen gray eyes, broad forehead and powerful jaw. His temperament is buoyant and youthful, and his physical endurance and ready interest are remarkable. His hair has now turned gray, but that is the only indication of advancing years. He was blessed with a sound constitution, and this, added to the fact that he eschewed the vices of youth and followed the path of manly rectitude and healthy recreation, has largely contributed to his success. Mr. Carnegie is a non-smoker, and exceedingly abstemious in his habits. Moderation in all things has characterized his mode of living and to this must be attributed his wonderful vitality of mind and body, which is superior to that possessed by many men half his age. Like Mr. Gladstone, the grand old man of the nineteenth century, whom he so reverently admired, Mr. Carnegie possesses the precious quality of being able to fall asleep at will, and in the short intervals between the stress of business he has a habit of dropping off into a refreshing slumber.

The retired capitalist speaks rather slowly and clearly enunciates every word. The maxim, "Think twice before you speak once," has great weight with him. He is not one to be led unawares into making a promise or expressing an opinion. He regards his interrogator with a keen look from his brilliant, shrewd, piercing eyes that seem to penetrate one's very mind ; then, even if it be merely a commonplace, he will answer in his deliberate way, clearly impressing his meaning upon his hearers. His face is a study in character. His large, penetrating eyes, broad fore- head and square chin stamp him as a man of commercial foresight, intellectual strength and strong will power. His features, though prominently marked, are not harsh in outline, or they would belie the genial blood which courses through his veins. Smiles are far more fashionable with Mr. Carnegie than scowls, though at times tie can look austere. He prefers optimism's blue skies to pessimism's dark caverns, and is always willing to exchange a joke or initiate a discussion. He is a clever conversationalist, with a ready command of reliable information and a good stock of stories drawn from his personal experience. His vocabulary is not limited, either, and when satisfied that his views are just he is not easily dislodged from his position. He has conversed with the great men of England and America, and wherever he goes he leaves the impression of a strongly welded character and a well-balanced mind.

In sharp contrast to his speech, his manner is very restless and indicative of a large reserve of pent-up energy, AU who have come in contact with the man have been impressed with his strong character and conspicuous ability. Ian Maclaren says of him, that the first time they met he felt instinctively that "an able-bodied, able-minded, fully equipped and well-finished man was there." Although short in stature, Mr. Carnegie has a large head, and unlike the brain that has amassed his millions, the hand that signs them away is small.

His office in his home, where he transacts his business, is fitted up with every convenience. His reservoir of information is a big chest of drawers, and each one is devoted to a separate object. Every drawer has affixed to it a label, such as "The Carnegie Steel Company's Reports, etc., etc.," "Correspondence about Libraries," "Grants, and Other Donations," "Applications for Aid," "Autograph Letters to Keep," "Publication Articles," "Skibo Estate," "Pittsburgh Institute." The indispensable typewriter is there as a matter of course, and hanging on the wall are a number of maps dotted with little flags to denote where the scene of action for the moment lies. Apart from an avalanche of wordy epistles, he has a large amount of business to transact, but he has an excellent system of rapid working, and with his capable secretary, Mr. James Bertram, he manages to accomplish his daily duties without seriously curtailing his leisure.

The Laird of Skibo is an omnivorous reader, and keeps himself thoroughly well informed on current affairs. Every day he reads half a dozen newspapers, and he digests a number of weeklies and all the important monthly reviews and magazines. Quick to single out what interests him, he ignores the rest. Of more solid literature he has read widely, and has a natural taste for the best writings of all ages. Shakespeare and Burns are his special favorites, and he pays each his daily homage by reading some portion of their works.

As his book, "Round the World," proves, Mr. Carnegie has traveled widely, and to some purpose.

He has crossed the Atlantic more than sixty times, and made expeditions to the North Cape, China, Japan, and Mexico. These extensive travels have widened the horizon of his thought and enriched his experience. His course through life has admirably fitted him for the great and responsible task he has set himself to fulfil. It can be truthfully said that, take him all in aU, there is no living person better fitted than himself to distribute his wealth wisely.

The task seems almost superhuman in its vastness, as every gift will be preceded by much thought and careful inquiry. Mr. Carnegie could give his fortune away at once, but one thing is certain, that no part of his wealth will be squandered in hasty and ill-advised gifts. If he kept his capital intact, which is most unlikely, and distributed his income alone in benefactions, he would be able to give away over $35,000 every day, or $13,750,000 per annum.

But no one knows through what channels Mr. Carnegie's wealth will flow, for he is not given to advertising his plans on the housetops before they are ready to be put in operation. Let it suffice us to know that he will fulfil his promise, and let us be thankful that such a vast agency for good is in the hands of a man actuated by the highest principles and the noblest ideals.